In case of loss, please return to:

_____

_____

_____

_____

As a reward: $_____

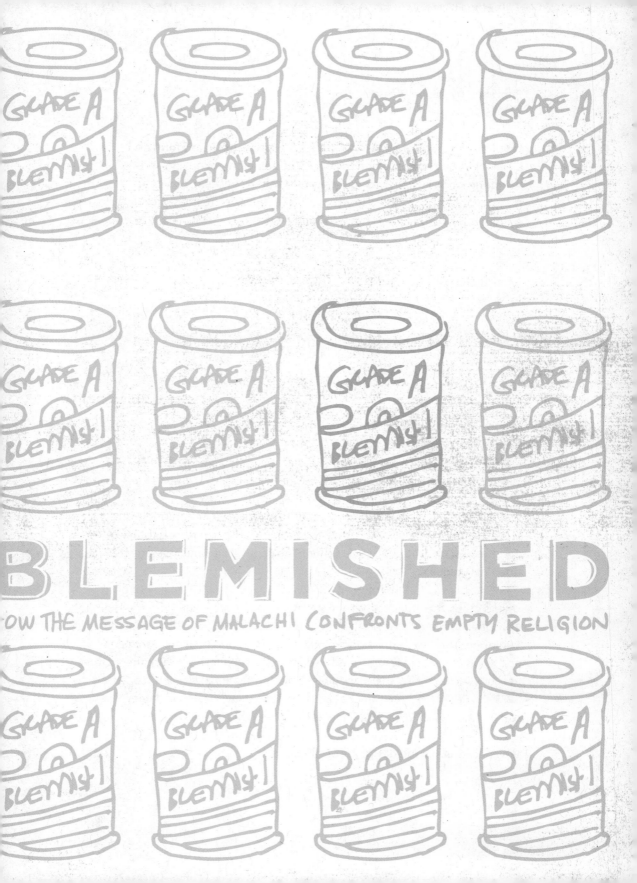

BLEMISHED

OW THE MESSAGE OF MALACHI CONFRONTS EMPTY RELIGION

Published by LifeWay Press®
© 2009 LifeWay Press®

ISBN: 978-1415-8665-04
Item: P005184405

Dewey Decimal Classification Number: 231.7
Subject Heading: GOD \ BIBLE. O.T. MALACHI--STUDY \ CHRISTIAN LIFE

Printed in the United States of America.

Leadership and Adult Publishing
LifeWay Church Resources
One LifeWay Plaza
Nashville, Tennessee 37234-0175

We believe the Bible has God for its author; salvation for its end; and truth,
without any mixture of error, for its matter and that all Scripture is totally true
and trustworthy. The 2000 statement of The Baptist Faith and Message is our
doctrinal guideline.

Unless otherwise indicated, all Scripture quotations are taken from the Holman
Christian Standard Bible®, copyright © 1999, 2000, 2002, 2003 by Holman Bible
Publishers. Used by permission. Holman Christian Standard Bible®, Holman CSB®,
and HCSB® are federally registered trademarks of Holman Bible Publishers. Other
versions include: NIV, the Holy Bible, New International Version, copyright ©
1973, 1978, 1984 by International Bible Society; NKJV, New King James Version,
copyright © 1979, 1980, 1982, Thomas Nelson, Inc., Publishers.

Cover illustration and design by Micah Kandros.

TABLE OF
CONTENTS

MEET THE AUTHOR

My name is Jason Hayes. I live in Hendersonville, Tennessee, and am happily married to my beautiful wife, Carrie. I'm also a proud dad to our son, Hayden. I serve as a voice and face for Threads, LifeWay's Young Adult initiative. My primary role for Threads is to serve as a speaker, church consultant, and writer.

I earned a Master of Divinity from The Southern Baptist Theological Seminary, and my love for learning expands into many realms of academia and culture. Before seminary, I attended the University of Tennessee where I earned a degree in speech communication. GO VOLS!

I've served in various roles over the years in both church and parachurch ministries. Prior to coming to LifeWay, I served at Long Hollow Church in north Nashville, where my responsibilities included teaching, spiritual growth, and much more. Although I'm now serving with Threads, our family is still active at Long Hollow.

I have been blessed to minister in North America, Africa, Asia, and Europe. I also have spoken at churches, conferences, training events, camps, retreats, university chapels, school assemblies, and various other venues around the country.

Our family enjoys spending time together and hanging out with the rest of our family and friends. I love ice cream, exercising, and spending as much time at the beach as possible. I also blog at *jasonhayesonline.com*.

Thanks for your willingness to journey alongside me through the Book of Malachi. I hope that you find as much joy in engaging this study as I had in writing it. May you find yourself encouraged, challenged, and propelled toward a deeper walk with Christ.

An **Unshakable** Idea

Have you ever had an idea that you just couldn't shake? You know the kind, right? Unshakable ideas are far from normal, everyday thoughts. Instead, these are the ideas that keep you awake at night. They're the ones that make your heart beat quickly. These are the ideas that drive you out of your present-day mindset and delve you into a world of vision and discovery. They excite you and yet terrify you at the same time because they're bigger than you are.

Some days you want to tell everyone about them, and other days you just need to process them by yourself. These are the ideas that send you beyond the grips of comfort and thrust you into the unknown. These ideas laugh in the face of apathy and combat the presence of mediocrity.

Well, I've got one, and this book is a dissection of that idea I just can't seem to shake. The idea is this: *What would happen if Christians actually made God preeminent in their lives?* I guess that's more of a question, so what about this: *The greatest revival in the history of the world could occur if Christians were actually obedient to God.* That's not too complicated an idea, right? After all, isn't that the entire concept behind Christianity—whole-hearted commitment to the God who made Himself available to His children through the redeeming blood of Jesus?

How have we managed to depart from such a clear calling? It seems like we've chosen to be selective when it comes to faith matters and the absence of such a revival is the result. Many Christians accept only certain parts of Scripture, primarily the ones that fit with their own desires and agree with mainstream culture. For others, a lack of beliefs is not the problem. Instead, the difficulty is found in the selective nature of what they'll choose to actually apply to their lives. They adamantly stand for the inerrancy and infallibility of Scripture (as do I), but they still choose to disregard all the parts in it that demand things such as repentance and obedience. So while the idea is one that's easy to understand, it's also one that isn't being executed.

This idea isn't original; it certainly didn't start with me. I'm the author of this book, but not this idea. It's God's idea, and so the purpose of this book isn't to promote the ingenuity of me or anyone else. Both this book and the idea behind it are God-breathed and God-focused. The idea is supernatural in origin and its intent is His glory. Because of its nature, it surfaces in my intimate times with the Lord and yet goes noticeably silent in my times of distance from Him.

I think I've always felt that a revival could, and would, occur if we were to really start living in radical obedience to God.

I think I've always felt that a revival could, and would, occur if we were to really start living in radical obedience to God. But I don't think I've ever seen that idea described more clearly than in the pages of the Old Testament book of Malachi. Several years ago I taught a sermon series from this little prophecy that closes out the Old Testament.

Malachi wasn't a book I spent much time in before that. Quite honestly, I'm not sure I had ever done anything besides zip through it in a Bible reading plan or an Old Testament course in seminary. But, for some reason, the Lord brought me back to it with a new interest during that time. I was fascinated by the nature of Malachi's message and the thought of God's silence toward entire generations of people.

And, ultimately, I was overwhelmed with conviction as I grasped my own responsibilities within a modern-day priesthood. As you'll see in the following pages, Malachi had a lot to say about the people of Israel, the Levitical priesthood, and their shortcomings. And, sadly, the more I examined Malachi's rebuke upon them, the more I saw myself in their lives. I not only saw my own life within their skewed proceedings, but I also saw a mindset toward the things of God and the church that looked dreadfully similar to much of what surrounded me.

Ever since that time, I've not been able to shake the rebuke of Malachi. I'm continually haunted by its parallels to our current state of spirituality. As you'll see, Malachi is not for light and fluffy leisure reading. I hope this study isn't either. In fact, I pray that the sting of Malachi's message would capture you in such a way that your life would never be the same after studying it. I earnestly believe that God would be pleased if you made this much more than a pure academic exercise. Instead, I urge you to allow its teaching to penetrate the innermost parts of your soul. I pray that you would mature in your faith as you grow in understanding of what that means.

As you'll see, it's quite clear what God's thoughts were of Israel and its priests. There was little room for confusion—God had laid out a framework of what He desired and they chose to distort it. He was displeased and He was direct. He was stern and yet He also continued to remind them of His love affair with them. In knowing that God is never changing (yet constantly relevant), we could conclude that He may have similar thoughts toward many of us today.

I hope that you walk away understanding that pleasing God is as much about the presence of obedience in our lives as it is the absence of blatant disobedience.

I hope you walk away understanding that pleasing God is as much about the presence of obedience in our lives as it is the absence of blatant disobedience. We all too often define our spiritual health by what we are doing wrong. But, as you'll see in Malachi, an evaluation of what we are not doing right is also necessary.

I don't know your circumstances or your shortcomings. Even if I did, it's not my place to judge or criticize you. However, please let me make this very clear—God has that right. I know that as a society we often push back on this type of correction, but in this context, it should be welcomed. I doubt that the people of Israel welcomed the rebuke they received from God through His prophet, Malachi. But, unfortunately, they couldn't see the motive behind it—God's loving efforts to draw them into a deeper, more intimate relationship with Himself. Let's not make this mistake.

As we journey together through these next several sessions, I would guess that you might see plenty of need for changes in your life. Please don't be discouraged by these things. Deal with them as needed—I can't stress that enough. But in the process, never lose sight of His passionate affection for you.

① REBUKED
A PROPHET'S WORDS—THEN AND NOW

A SACRIFICE ISN'T SOMETHING YOU JUST STUMBLE ONTO. It's not a flippant party or an event you can casually observe. Take the biggest sacrifice of the Jewish calendar, for instance.

The Day of Atonement came after ten intentional days of repentance and reflection, of confession and introspection. Those "Ten Days of Awe" set the stage for the sacrifice, and with that much anticipation and buildup, the sacrifice to God was undeniably meaningful. It was serious, wonderful, and fearful, all at the same time.

The temple sat on a small mountain called Mount Zion, and every year hundreds of thousands gathered there for the sacrifices. A choir of hundreds sang accompanied by hundreds of musicians, while priests led prayers and attended to sacrificial duties. Each year there was a sense of both expectation and dread, because the sacrifice reminded everyone of who God is and who they had failed to be.

ANCIENT REBUKE, MODERN CHURCH

I love the church. And I believe in the church. I believe in the authority of Scripture, and so I believe what it says about the church. I believe that the church will survive despite the many obstacles it faces in today's culture, and that the church will always exist. Through the work of the Holy Spirit, I believe that it is the primary vehicle by which God desires to reveal His glory to the world.

I also believe, however, that the church is wrongly defined and extraordinarily misunderstood by many. I believe that all too often we've defined the church to be a physical building of bricks and mortar as opposed to the body of believers who gather there. These people are what make me love the church. They, not our buildings and programs, are what make it worth loving.

How would you define "the church"?

How necessary is the church to your life? How do you think God feels about the church?

I also believe that most non-Christians stand on the outside of our faith communities with inaccurate perceptions as to what the church is and wonder why on earth they would have any need for it. Oh sure, most people, regardless of whether they're Christians or not, want something "spiritual" in their lives, but they're far more likely to turn to Oprah, or Hollywood, or inside themselves than to darken the doors of a church. To quote Dan Kimball, "they like Jesus but not the church."[1]

How do you think most people outside the church feel about it?

"Christianity means community through Jesus Christ and in Jesus Christ. No Christian community is more or less than this. Whether it be a brief, single encounter or the daily fellowship of years, Christian community is only this. We belong to one another only through and in Jesus Christ."
– Dietrich Bonhoeffer

The New Testament word for church is *ekklesia*, and it was originally used to describe an assembly of citizens who were "called out" by a herald. The biblical meaning, then, is a group of earthly people who have been called out by Christ for His purposes.[2]

What about inside the church? How do you think most of those people feel about it?

What do you think the major influences are for people's opinions of the church?

It's true that people's rejection of the church is partly a result of various "x-factors," such as poor experiences in the past, exposure to false teachings, and the broad impact of mainstream media. But I also believe that much of the blame for this misunderstanding can be placed firmly on the shoulders of Christians themselves. It's our fault they want Jesus but not the church. It's no big secret as we gaze across the landscape of "churchdom" that there's a lot going wrong.

What's interesting to me is that the problems we have in the church aren't exactly new. We struggle to have an authentically deep relationship with the Lord where we truly love Him rather than just perform perfunctory religious duties. We struggle to take care of those around us because we're consumed with meeting our own desires. We struggle to bring our best to the Lord rather than what is left over. And we struggle to articulate our faith and stand for truth in the midst of a culture that frowns on anything claiming to be "absolute."

So did our parents. So did their parents. So did their parents before them and so on, all the way back to the Old Testament. Before there were church buildings or programs, before there were denominations or factions, the chosen people of God were struggling with many of the same things the church is dealing with today.

And during those days, there was a prophet ready to hand down a rebuke—a ringing condemnation—from heaven. Meet Malachi.

This very significant (although often overlooked) character from the Bible gave us a book of Scripture dedicated to uncovering and dealing with many of the same issues that hound the 21st century Christ follower. Though Malachi's words weren't initially directed toward us, there's much to be learned from this ancient rebuke.

Dan Kimball oversees the Sunday worship gatherings and teaching of Vintage Faith Church in Santa Cruz, Calif. He is the author of several books including *They Like Jesus but Not the Church.*

According to *lifewayresearch. com,* though 71 percent of unchurched Americans said they believed Jesus "makes a positive difference in a person's life," a full 72 percent said they think the church "is full of hypocrites."

John Piper, speaking about the message of Malachi, said: "To this carnal and rebellious people God sent His messenger . . . and the first message he put on his lips was, 'I have loved you, says the Lord!'" For more of Piper's sermons, visit *desiringgod.org.*

How do you feel about the word "rebuke"?

When was the last time you were rebuked for something?

What sort of rebuke would Malachi deliver if he lived today?

WHO IS MALACHI?

The book of the Bible is called Malachi because he's the one who wrote it. But some scholars have suggested that Malachi, a name meaning "my messenger," or "the LORD's messenger," could simply be a title instead of someone's name. Adding to this idea is the fact that the name Malachi doesn't appear anywhere else in the Old Testament.[3]

I'm led to believe that Malachi is actually the name of the writer of the book because it's included in the prophetic writings of the Old Testament. These books, such as Isaiah, Jeremiah, Hosea, Amos, and others, all follow the same general pattern. In the introduction, the name of the prophet is explicitly listed and introduced to the audience. That's why most scholars agree that Malachi was the actual author's name of this final book of the Old Testament.

Most also conclude that Malachi was likely written around the fifth century B.C., probably between 433–424, about the same time as Nehemiah's return to Persia. You can place the writing of Malachi in this time period by comparing the historical timeline with several events and happenings that we'll be discussing in the pages to come, but here are a few to start with:

Sacrifices had resumed at the temple, a practice restarted by Ezra and Nehemiah after the exiled Jews returned to their homeland. Malachi prophesied several years after this happened. Apparently, as those years had gone by, both the priests and the people had forgotten the significance behind the sacrificial system they were adhering to. Sure, they still participated, but they had become hardened to the things of

Scholars who don't believe Malachi is a proper name argue that the same word is translated as "my messenger" in Malachi 3:1. Malachi 2:7 also refers to priests as God's "messengers." They believe, therefore, that the name *Malachi* "describes the anonymous agent who will be sent to prepare the way for God's future coming."[4]

God and following His law. Their religious actions had become a checklist rather than something they did in loving obedience. They saw these actions as a kind of permission slip to live as they pleased, because after all, God would forgive them for anything if they just offered the sacrifice.[5]

When you think about offering sacrifices, what images come to mind?

Can you identify anything similar to these acts in your own religious tradition?

In addition to the Jews' sin issues, they were becoming even more hardened and jaded in their hearts. For years they learned about their history as a nation, how God had made huge promises to Abraham and David, and how He promised to institute a new covenant with His people. They knew those things, but they were still waiting for them to happen. Simply, they were in worse shape than ever before and had yet to see their long-awaited Messiah.

Read Malachi 1:6-14. What is most striking to you in this passage?

What was God's complaint against the Israelites? What is the emotion behind their response?

Why do you think the sacrificial system was so important to God?

Malachi returned to Judah from Persia after the Israelites were exiled there. The return was around 433 B.C. His prophecies most likely fit between Nehemiah's two residences in Jerusalem. This would place him as a prophet about 100 years after Haggai and Zechariah.[6]

The Hebrew word used to express the concept of covenant is *berit*. The original meaning was "fetter" or "obligation," coming from a root meaning "to bind." The word emphasizes the unalterable and permanent quality of the agreement.

Malachi had these thoughts in mind as he delivered his message to the nation. But as was the case with all the prophets, he wasn't just passing out a personal "beat-down" to the people; he was penning the words of God. Just as Christ wrote what He thought about the condition of the churches in the Book of Revelation, God wrote through Malachi to express His thoughts toward the nation of Israel in the final book of the Old Testament. Malachi wrote this prophecy in order to deliver the bad news—due to their refusal to turn from their sin, the people of Israel were going to incur the judgment of God.[7]

But even in the midst of the bad news, God reminded His people through Malachi of something very, very good—a day was coming in the future when all of God's promises would be fulfilled. The coming Messiah would lead God's people into the fullness of fellowship with Him.[8]

So Malachi was tasked to deliver a whole lot of bad news with splotches of hope mixed in. To effectively communicate his message, Malachi chose to make his point in the form of an imagined dialogue between God and the people. As you read Malachi, you'll notice that he used lots of questions and answers to communicate his prophecy. Much of the time, this dispute takes the form of God asking a question and the people of Israel answering Him, usually in cynical fashion. This back and forth goes on throughout the book, with Malachi picturing himself as God's spokesman. Like a lawyer in court, the prophet posed rhetorical questions meant to cut to the heart of the people, even in the midst of their opposition.

Do you feel like you question God more or He questions you more? Why?

What sort of questions do you imagine God might have for you?

WHY MALACHI?

You don't have to get very far into Malachi to see that God wasn't happy with very many people. Although part of Malachi's rebuke is related to the people of Israel (2:10-16), a greater majority of the text is dedicated to his rebuke of Israel's priests (1:6–2:9). Now maybe your

---

"'For indeed, the day is coming, burning like a furnace, when all the arrogant and everyone who commits wickedness will become stubble. The coming day will consume them,' says the LORD of Hosts, 'not leaving them root or branches. But for you who fear My name, the sun of righteousness will rise with healing in its wings, and you will go out and playfully jump like calves from the stall'" (Malachi 4:1-2).

The same form of question and answer can be found in a number of different places in Scripture, including Habakkuk. In Habakkuk, however, the prophet was asking legitimate questions of God.

eyebrows just rose a little bit, and you've got a slightly quizzical look on your face. You're thinking, *If this is mainly about priests, why am I reading about it?*

That's a legitimate question, but why stop there? We're also not offering sacrifices any more, and lots of Malachi is about that. We're not part of the people of Israel, and much of the Old Testament is about that. And we live in a post-Christ, post-Pentecost world where we don't need prophets anymore; we can hear from God ourselves. Why study these things at all?

So what do you think? What relationship do we as 21st century Christ followers have to the priests of Israel?

For that matter, what relationship do we have to the Old Testament? What value is there in studying texts written to people prior to the coming of Christ?

All good questions. Answering those questions is what makes the study of the Old Testament so rewarding but also somewhat difficult at times. Take the issue we began with, for instance. The question was about priests. If we turn back further into the Old Testament, we find that the priests of Israel served as the intermediaries between the people and God. They were the go-betweens, and part of their job as go-betweens was to offer sacrifices to the Lord on behalf of the people. But as the spiritual authorities of the land they were also tasked with introducing people to the ways of God. They were the middlemen and the only people who had access to both people and God.

As you come to the New Testament, the priestly imagery is really important because, among other titles, Jesus is described as our Great High Priest (Hebrews 3 and 4). He is the last priest and now the only one needed between us and God. He is the final bridge, the relationship mediator between humanity and divinity. With Him as our intercessor, we have direct access to God. No more going through a priestly or sacrificial system in order to relate to the Almighty; Jesus took care of that once and for all. Period.

Reverberations of Faith: A Theological Handbook of Old Testament Themes by Walter Brueggemann provides a concise and well-organized view of the most important themes in the Old Testament, including priests, priestly duties, and sacrifices. It's a great reference tool to keep on your Bible study shelf.

"For there is one God and one mediator between God and man, a man, Christ Jesus, who gave Himself—a ransom for all, a testimony at the proper time" (1 Timothy 2:5-6).

What are the implications of knowing Jesus as the Great High Priest?

In his essay "Christian Ministry," J.B. Lightfoot expanded the Christian doctrine known as the priesthood of all believers. Lightfoot wrote that "as individuals, all Christians are priests alike." He continued to say: "The most exalted office in the Church, the highest gift of the Spirit, conveyed no sacerdotal right which was not enjoyed by the humblest member of the Christian community."[9]

What does that fact do to our access to God?

Because of what Jesus has done, all Christ followers are priests now. We all have the same access to God that once was limited to a select few.

That's very important for us to realize because of the implications it has for a modern reading of Malachi. We've said already that much of Malachi's criticism rests on the priests of Israel; and yet here we are in the 21st century, as priests ourselves. That means we, as priests, would do well to read carefully the biting words the prophet uttered centuries ago.

Have you ever thought of yourself as a priest? What responsibilities go along with a designation like that?

Are you comfortable with that title? Why or why not?

The priests of Israel were responsible for two major things. First, they were responsible for teaching the Law of Moses. Second, they were called to be a reflection of God's glory. As you seek to find parallels in how all of this relates to you, it's important to be reminded that you are called to be faithful in similar ways. You are called to honor God with your life and strive to live out the instruction you find in His Word, the Bible.

DIVINE SILENCE

The Book of Malachi is probably best known for being the last book in the Old Testament. This is significant. For centuries God had been communicating with His people verbally through prophets. He spoke to men such as Isaiah, Jeremiah, Ezekiel, Hosea, and Malachi through voices, dreams, and visions, and they delivered His messages to the people. The land of Israel seemed to always have the words, "Thus sayeth the Lord …" ringing throughout it as these prophets were faithful mouthpieces of God.

But then, after Malachi, there was nothing. Israel experienced more than 400 years of divine silence—with only Malachi's words echoing in their ears—before another prophet arrived with a message from God. Again, this isn't just a small "fun fact" that should be passed over quickly. Take a moment and grasp the implication of this silence. It wasn't that God was absent or that He was dead. Instead, He went purposefully quiet.

Nothing. No angels, dreams, visions, symbolic actions, gentle whispers, miraculous signs, or prophetic messengers. Absolute silence. It kind of makes you wonder—knowing that He was going to go silent, what was the last thing God wanted to say to His people before the time of Christ?

What is significant to you about the 400 years of silence?

Have you ever felt you experienced a period of divine silence like this? What were the circumstances?

The period between the Old and New Testaments is called the intertestamental period. Though the Bible doesn't contain writings from that period, a tremendous amount of historical change occurred in those 400 years. The land of Israel was occupied first by the Greeks, then by the Romans, each threatening the national and religious identity of the Hebrews. And while these specific events aren't documented in Scripture, the Book of Daniel has remarkably accurate predictions related to those world happenings.

The problem is that Malachi ends the Old Testament not with a blessing but with the warning of a curse. The four short chapters from the mouth of the prophet instill in us a feeling of despair, because if we're honest with ourselves, we know that we're never going to be able to put forward an unblemished offering. We'll never be clean enough. We'll never be pure enough. In truth, even our best intentions are tainted with selfish, prideful, or misguided motives. The whole Book of Malachi is about presenting unblemished offerings before God, and yet we can't do it. It's as if God is calling us to do—and be—something that is impossible for us to do and be.

Four hundred years is a long time to live with that. And yet we know this was an intentional word from the Lord, because no other word was capable of setting up what was coming four centuries later.

How do you reconcile the fact that God was calling His people to something impossible?

Have you ever felt like He was doing something similar to you? In what sense?

The temple was intended to be the center of religious life for Israel, a place where God dwelt in the middle of His people. Coming to the temple was coming to a meeting with God, one in which a person expected an encounter with the holy.

THE IMPORTANCE OF SACRIFICE

For 400 years, the people lived with God's lingering warning and condemnation. And yet, through those long years, they persisted in the same half-hearted commitment to the sacrificial system that had gotten them so much criticism from the Lord.

In fact, life in Israel revolved around the temple and the sacrificial system that operated there. The priests served in the temple, which means they were responsible for performing very specific rituals designed to honor God by presenting offerings to Him. One of the primary elements in these rituals was the presentation and sacrifice of animals. It was absolutely vital that the priests presented very specific animals in very specific ways. Scripture required the sacrifice to be the absolute best animal available. The animal couldn't be blind or lame or crippled or diseased. It needed to be an unblemished offering, a perfect sacrifice.[10]

The significance of such an offering is fairly obvious—it's an expression of one's love, devotion, and obedience to God. By giving their best, a person signifies their belief in the worth and supremacy of God, that He deserves the absolute best they have. But it's also an expression of faith.

Why would God demand the absolute best sacrifice available?

How is the offering of such a sacrifice an expression of faith?

When someone is willing to give their first and best to the Lord, an offering that could be used to make money or provide for their family, they are expressing their belief that the Lord will provide if they only trust in Him. Faith is about choosing to believe rather than acting on your own behalf. That sacrifice could have been used for financial gain, but instead, the people were to offer it, believing in God's ability to bless and provide.

THE ULTIMATE SACRIFICE

The image of the sacrifice runs right through the Mosaic law and into the New Testament, and that's where we pick up after 400 quiet years. Finally, and abruptly, God started speaking again. Four hundred years later, John the Baptist arrived on the scene. And he had the feel of one of the prophets of old. Let's face it—prophets have a weird vibe. So did John. He was the one hanging out in the wilderness wearing crazy stuff like camel's hair. He was also the one who snacked on locusts and wild honey. But more importantly, he spoke the prophetic message of repentance and a call toward righteousness:

"Repent, because the kingdom of heaven has come near!" (Matthew 3:2).

John also made baptism a part of his message. Although John's baptism was connected to Old Testament ritual, it was still a symbol of repentance. While repentance is certainly an element of Christian baptism today, it now also represents the death, burial, and resurrection of Jesus.

Speaking of Jesus, that's who John the Baptist was all about. More specifically, he was preaching the good news of Jesus Christ's coming. Consider John the Baptist's response when, as he was preaching and baptizing at the edge of the Jordan River, he looked up and saw Jesus approaching. He didn't say, "Here comes Jesus!" or "Get ready, the King is on His way!" Instead, he returned immediately to the familiar metaphor of the sacrificial system that had been around for centuries:

"The next day John saw Jesus coming toward him and said, 'Here is the Lamb of God, who takes away the sin of the world!'" (John 1:29).

The Hebrew word translated as "unblemished" comes from *tamam*, meaning "whole." The wholeness can be literal, figurative, or moral. To be unblemished is to lack nothing in any sense.[11]

John was the son of Zechariah the priest and Elizabeth. His birth was foretold by an angel, and his coming was the fulfillment of the expectation of the return of Elijah. John's message can be boiled down to two important points: the coming of the messianic kingdom and the urgent need for repentance in light of that event. You can read more about him in Luke 1:57-80 and John 1:19-36.

What is significant about the way John described Jesus?

In what sense was Jesus a sacrifice?

"Since the law has only a shadow of the good things to come, and not the actual form of those realities, it can never perfect the worshipers by the same sacrifices they continually offer year after year. ... For it is impossible for the blood of bulls and goats to take away sins" (Hebrews 10:1,4).

It's extraordinarily significant that Jesus is identified as "the Lamb of God" here. This imagery would've been recognized immediately by a Jewish audience, since the Old Testament is full of descriptions of how a lamb was to be used as a sacrifice. Exodus 12:1-36 prescribes a lamb to be "used as a sacrifice during Passover." We also see that "a lamb was led to slaughter" in Isaiah 53:7 and that "a lamb was offered in the daily sacrifices of Israel" in passages like Leviticus 14:12-21 and Hebrews 10:5-7. Similar daily offerings were also required of the priests of Israel during the days of Malachi. But John the Baptist was using this familiar imagery in a new and ultimately final way. He was referring to Jesus as the last Lamb ... the final sacrifice.[12]

Even from the beginning of His ministry, Christ was identified as a sacrifice. But He wasn't going to be just any sacrifice. See, the sacrificial system was leading up to and foreshadowing the sacrifice of Christ. And in that foreshadowing, there was special emphasis put on the perfection of the sacrifice. This was meant to be a clear picture of what was coming, for Jesus truly had no spot or blemish. He was completely clean, absolutely without sin. First Peter 2:22 says, "He did not commit sin, and no deceit was found in His mouth." First John 3:5 says, "There is no sin in Him."

God went into extensive detail regarding the nature of the sacrifices His people were to offer, and in that intricate explanation, He made it clear that the sacrificial lamb was to be free from imperfections. The same thing is true of Jesus in His sacrificial role. But whereas the lambs were considered unblemished if they were without spot or stain, Jesus had to be clean both inside and out. In order to atone for our sins, He had to be completely spotless on the inside. He could have no stray thoughts, no double-minded intention, and no secret ill will. Only such a sacrifice could truly take away our sin.

Jesus had to live up to a perfect level of righteousness that included abstaining from evil, but that standard of righteousness also included doing good always, even in the onset of persecution, or the entire plan would fail! So Jesus was not only the fulfillment of the Old Testament prophecy—He was the provision of the ultimate "perfect sacrifice" that would provide atonement between a perfect God and fallen man. He was and is our unblemished offering.

That's huge. It's bigger than huge. While it's world-changing for us, consider how much more amazing it was for the people who found themselves in the midst of 400 years of divine silence. They were left with despair—a sense of total hopelessness—and then God comes bursting onto the scene again with a message of grace and redemption.

The 400-year absence accentuates the goodness of Christ. After being silent for so long, this new Lamb, the final Lamb, is God's ultimate word on sacrifices. It is His final proclamation of mercy and grace to a world that can never be good enough.

> **What implications does His sacrifice have for the entire sacrificial system?**

> **How does God expect us to live in light of the sacrifice of Christ?**

Christopher Wright has written *Knowing Jesus Through the Old Testament* under the premise that Jesus Christ is the central character of Scripture. Pick up a copy to find His starring role in the Old Testament as well as the New.

ALREADY ACCEPTABLE . . .

That's good news, isn't it? The truth is that as priests, we are often guilty of the same things that got the priests reamed by Malachi. The issue with the priests wasn't just the actual, physical offerings they brought. Those often were physically blemished, but they were also blemished because the spirit behind them was blemished, too. The priests brought inappropriate offerings because they had inappropriate hearts. These heart issues lie at the center of God's rebuke.

Likewise, we often bring blemished offerings before God—a lack of commitment, half-hearted worship, grudging generosity, and bitter obedience. Sure, we bring offerings, but our hearts are spotty at best. We might do the right thing, but do it with the entirely wrong heart.

Listen to "Connecting with Malachi—Part I" as author Jason Hayes discusses some additional implications from the Book of Malachi. Your group leader will send it to you via e-mail.

Take a moment and think about what initially comes to mind as you think about your life as an offering to God. Are you clean or unclean? Are you blemished or unblemished?

Have you ever tried to clean yourself up? What was the result?

"He made the One who did not know sin to be sin for us, so that we might become the righteousness of God in Him" (2 Corinthians 5:21).

When you meet with your small group this week, watch "Why Goats Matter to Me," a video short found on the *Blemished* leader kit. Think through what the sacrificial system of the Old Testament means to the 21st century Christ follower.

Well, before you beat yourself up too badly and get overly discouraged by your inevitable future shortcomings, take a moment and be encouraged in your identity as a Christ follower. This is a really important point that can also serve as a word of caution for you as you begin this study. Hear this: You will never be an acceptable or unblemished offering on your own.

However, in an amazing display of grace and mercy, we are given the chance to be found acceptable through the atoning work of Jesus Christ, despite our flawed and insufficient efforts to please God. On our own, our life as an "offering" would never be acceptable or unblemished. But if you are a Christ follower and know Him as Lord, here's the amazing truth—Jesus' life, death, and resurrection serves as the ultimate perfect sacrifice that you could never present to the Father on your own! We see in Ephesians 5:2 that we are to "walk in love, as the Messiah also loved us and gave Himself for us, a sacrificial and fragrant offering to God." Christ came to be the ultimate sacrifice and the ultimate offering.

. . . BUT CALLED TO OBEDIENCE

It's amazing to consider the fact that right now I'm not trying to be righteous before God—I already am. God looks at me and sees the righteousness of Christ. But that truth begs the question: If what we've seen in Scripture thus far is true and we are found unblemished in the eyes of God, then why would we need to evaluate our lives, and why would we need to learn from the words of Malachi anyway? For that matter, why would we need to follow God's direction at all?

Maybe we should go back and look at the Levitical priests for our answer. As previously mentioned, the priests were responsible for teaching the law *and* displaying the glory of God. Although you may know God and the work of Christ in your life is now seen as an unblemished offering, you are still called to be obedient to Him who has redeemed you. We've got to avoid the pitfall that has trapped Christianity for centuries—the trap of being grace-abusers. If we look at Christ's work in our lives as a permission slip for our conduct, we become just like the people described in Jude 4: "They are ungodly, turning the grace of our God into promiscuity."

Why is it so easy to become a grace-abuser?

Have you ever felt yourself falling into this line of behavior? Why?

Jude was the brother of James and, more importantly, the brother of Jesus. Though Jesus' family failed largely to believe in His ministry when He was alive, His brothers became pillars in the church after His ascension to heaven. Jude was probably some kind of itinerate evangelist (1 Corinthians 9:5). He wrote his letter to address immoral conduct happening during Christian feasts.

The seriousness of obedience should be emphasized again as we look back to the Levitical priests. They had a responsibility to God, but they also had a responsibility to the people of Israel.

So here's the bottom line for many of us: Although we're seen as acceptable offerings in the eyes of God, we may be pointing those around us completely away from God because of how we're living. When you think about it that way, it seems pretty selfish, doesn't it? Although others will never see us just as God sees us, they should be able to clearly see a life made different by His grace. The Levitical priests inaccurately represented the greatness and glory of God to a nation of people who were desperately looking to them to encounter Him.

This is the other role of the priests—to introduce those who don't know God to His ways. We do that by living in obedience to the words of Christ.

My prayer is that this study would help you grasp the significance of your life, your role as a priest. As you consider what type of offering your life is, may you learn from Malachi's rebuke, and strive to reflect Christ to a world desperately searching for God. We have been given the incredible responsibility of representing God in the world. That's what a priest has always done. But we would do well to ask ourselves what sort of picture are we putting out there for others to see?

REFLECTING ON MALACHI

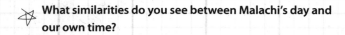

As you finish this session of *Blemished*, begin reading through the Book of Malachi. This week, focus on Malachi 1:1-5. It's a short passage, but spend some time reflecting on the following questions:

✮ **What similarities do you see between Malachi's day and our own time?**

✮ **How had the people disregarded the love of God?**

✮ **Do you see any similarities in the church today?**

✮ **What do you think about this book being God's last word to His people before the New Testament?**

In conjunction with your reading in Malachi, spend some time reading the Book of 2 Timothy in the New Testament. Focus particularly on verses 3:1-9.

✮ **What phrases stand out to you in this passage?**

✮ **What similarities do you see to Malachi?**

2 CRIPPLED ACTIONS

THE FAILURE TO CONNECT "WHAT" AND "WHEN"

THE PROCEDURE ON THE DAY OF ATONEMENT WAS AN INTRICATE ONE—one that had been practiced for centuries, and one that called for the utmost care. Imagine what must have gone through the mind of the high priest, the central figure of the day. The high priest was responsible for bringing the sacrifice before the Lord and representing the people as God judged their sins for another year.

He must have laid awake at night for weeks considering his responsibility and making sure he was prepared to translate all his knowledge into action. It was imperative he did so, and the rope tied around his waist reminded him why. If he failed to perform the sacrificial duties exactly as he was supposed to, he would die. If he failed to come out, the rope was the only way the people could remove his body from the Holy of Holies. The rope was there in case all the information about the sacrifice, everything he studied, all he rehearsed, the totality of what he learned—didn't make it from his head to his actions.

UNDERSTANDING ONLY GOES SO FAR

One of my favorite things about the church where I most recently served was the people. Not only do I love the people I served, but I also love the staff I served alongside. One of the most important activities each year was our staff retreat. It was a time for us to get away to plan, organize, and dream, but also have some laughs together.

One year our retreat was held at Horn's Creek, near the Ocoee River in east Tennessee. The retreat center was great and had all the necessary accommodations for us to accomplish what we needed over those few days. But the real highlight was the river itself.

Let's be clear about this fact—the Ocoee is a *river*. It's not a brook. It's not a stream. It's a river that has killed some and injured lots. For years, local outfitters have welcomed thrill-seeking rafters looking to experience the Ocoee River firsthand. This powerful waterway has miles of challenging and exciting Class III and IV rapids and is one of the country's premier rivers. The Ocoee's splashy waves and continuous action have earned it the nickname "Ocoee Coaster." The Middle Ocoee is the nation's most popular whitewater run, while the Upper Ocoee boasts as the home of the 1996 Olympic Whitewater competition. I'm not exaggerating—some of the rapids are named things like Tablesaw, Broken Nose, Double Trouble, and Powerhouse.

As we arrived, our group broke into groups of five and six. These were the people with whom we'd be rafting the river that day. After a safety overview at the outpost, we all boarded a bus to begin our trek to the top of the river. The adrenaline started pumping.

When we got off the bus, the first order of business was to get more acquainted with our guide. She's who you really need to know, since she explains how to avoid dying or being horribly disfigured in a rafting accident. So we paid very close attention when she walked us through the various verbal instructions that she would be giving throughout our ride and how we were supposed to respond. We also took a few moments to practice various paddling techniques and directional maneuvers at the command of our guide. She gave us three basic rules:

Rule number one—hold on to the paddle, and hold on to it correctly. If we lost the paddles we couldn't steer. **Rule two**—listen to her and do what she says on the water. **Rule three**—sit correctly in the boat. Pretty simple, right? That's what I thought, so I was a little annoyed when she wanted to go through it all again. *Ugh. What does she think we're not getting?* After going back through these three instructions, she

To plan your own whitewater rafting adventure, check out *rafting.com*. You'll find links to destinations across the world, as well as descriptions of rapids and other information to help you plan for the trip.

went to each of us individually and asked, "Do you understand?" One by one we all signaled our understanding and then finally, after all of this buildup and anticipation, we were actually headed down river.

The very first rapids, which are within just a few hundred feet of the entry, also happen to be some of the strongest and biggest rapids on the river. But we had a great team, we were informed and prepped, and now we simply had to execute. And that's where the story goes all wrong.

When we were barely wet from the first splash, pandemonium broke out among us. The roar of the rapids had yet to even swallow us and our raft was still in good position, but I looked around and our team was freaking out. I looked over to my right and saw my friend doing just about everything possible with his paddle but holding onto it correctly. Instead, he was holding it like a guitar or a microphone or something. Either way, he wasn't doing what he was supposed to be doing. I started screaming at him, "Get your hand on the T-grip!"

Then I heard screaming coming from behind me. The guy was so excited he wasn't paying any attention to the commands of our guide. He certainly couldn't hear her instruction over his yelling; nor could anyone else on the raft. So now he too wasn't doing what he was supposed to be doing!

About that time, another member and I slipped off our seats into the boat bottom. No one on our entire team had done what we were asked to do. It was a disaster. Well, as you can imagine, we had a fun day. The first rapids weren't too great, but we managed to get through it alive. What's the point to be drawn out of all this?

I listened to the guide as she asked me, "Do you understand?" I affirmed yes. She asked everyone else the same question, and one by one we all had the same response. Despite that, we all failed to do what had been asked of us. Despite our understanding of what to do, we didn't execute what we'd committed to do. We had knowledge of what we were supposed to do, but when it came to application we fell short.

Is gaining knowledge or applying that knowledge more difficult for you? Why?

Listen to "Pass Me Not" by the Robbie Seay Band on the *Blemished* playlist. Your leader will send you the whole playlist via e-mail, or you can find it at *threadsmedia.com/media*. Use these songs as the background music for your study.

Why do you think so many of us stop at the knowledge and neglect the application?

KNOWLEDGE VERSUS APPLICATION

Most of us know a lot of stuff. We can quote everything from lines from "Seinfeld" to the Declaration of Independence to the occasional Bible verse thrown in here or there. But just like in the raft, there is a huge difference between knowledge and the application of that knowledge, especially in a spiritual sense. Knowledge without action leads only to pride. It's worthless. It's simply not enough for us to *know*; we must also *do*. This is a prominent issue that Malachi identifies in his rebuke of the Levitical priests, but it's also a common theme all throughout Scripture. And yet there is a huge disconnect between what we know and what we do.

What are some other consequences of accumulating knowledge and yet not applying it?

Why is that such a dangerous proposition?

"We know that 'we all have knowledge.' Knowledge inflates with pride, but love builds up" (1 Corinthians 8:1).

How about the opposite? What's the danger in applying truths without pursuing knowledge?

As we've established, much of Malachi's rebuke was aimed directly at the Levitical priests. But to see exactly why Malachi—and God—were so bent out of shape, we need to understand how far the priests had strayed from their required tasks. Passages like Numbers 3:44-48, Numbers 18:8-24, and Deuteronomy 33:8-11 clearly define what the relationship between God and these spiritual leaders was supposed to be like. With just a cursory reading, it seems the bargain was simple: God expected reverence for Himself in exchange for life and peace for the priest.

But the priests wanted to have it both ways. Rather than keeping their part of the covenant, they had convinced themselves they could claim the covenant's privileges while not choosing to follow its regulations. Malachi disagreed.

Read Malachi 2:1-9, then go back and read Malachi 1:6. What stands out the most to you in these passages?

What are some areas of your life where you want to "have it both ways"?

In the 2006 film *Stranger Than Fiction*, Will Ferrell plays a character learning the difference between head knowledge and real life. Just for fun, check out this movie with your small group.

These men were unfaithful to all that God was calling them to, but the problem went deeper than that. As the spiritual representatives of the people, their actions were leading an entire nation away from rightly following and worshiping God. That's why we see God clearly call out these priests in His rebuke:

"'A son honors his father, and a servant his master. But if I am a father, where is My honor? And if I am a master, where is your fear of Me? says the LORD of Hosts to you priests, who despise My name.' Yet you ask: 'How have we despised Your name?'" (Malachi 1:6).

You can't get much more direct than that. Though it's direct, it's not incredibly specific. The priests, however, were guilty in several very specific areas that led to this general rebuke. The Old Testament law went to painstaking lengths to make sure the priests were well-informed about the nature of their duties.

When you start reading the law, you find chapter after chapter detailing in minute ways the very specific responsibilities of the priests. Levitical priests served for 25 years, from age 25 to age 50 (Numbers 8:24,25). Exodus 29 records the extensive process by which someone was consecrated, or set apart, for a priestly role. During their service, their duties included: the teaching of the Law (Leviticus 10:11); offering the sacrifices (Leviticus 9); maintaining the tabernacle and the temple

(Numbers 18:3); officiating in the Holy Place (Exodus 30:7-10); and inspecting ceremonially unclean persons (Leviticus 13-14). What's more, they adjudicated disputes (Deuteronomy 17:8-13) and functioned as tax collectors (Numbers 18:21,26).

The Old Testament also sets apart one of the priests as the high priest, giving him even more specialized responsibilities. The principal duty of the high priest was to officiate on the Day of Atonement (Leviticus 16). When the high priest, wearing his ceremonial garments, drew near to God. He entered the tabernacle (or later the temple), and sprinkled blood from the unblemished sacrifice there. The blood was meant to be a sin offering for himself. Upon doing that, he would exit the Holy of Holies, only to re-enter to sprinkle the blood of a goat as a sin offering for the people.

How do you see the foreshadowing of Jesus in this system?

Why do you think God set up such an intricate system for sacrifices?

What does this intricacy reveal to you about God?

This system of sacrifices was meant to illustrate God's requirement of blood to pardon personal and corporate sin (Leviticus 16:30). We know from the New Testament that the whole process was also meant to be the initial picture of what Christ would eventually do on the cross (cf. Hebrews 5:1ff).

The directions were extensive. The requirements were specific. But more than anything, they were intentional. God wasn't simply handing down a jumbled set of unfair instructions; everything had a purpose and everything was symbolic. But possibly even more noteworthy than this, there was a great discipline and order within the execution of these practices. The duties of the priests were never decided

Aaron was the first high priest, instituted during the time when God made His covenant with Israel on Mount Sinai. Aaron was responsible for Israel's worship, the tabernacle, and the sacrifices and festivals. The office of the high priest and the priesthood was passed down on a hereditary basis.[13]

whimsically or just off the cuff. These rituals weren't up for adaptation or revision. There were extraordinarily high standards as to how each responsibility of the priesthood was to be performed. And the merit of each priest was closely connected to how they performed the responsibilities within this framework.

As you might imagine, ignorance was not an acceptable excuse. Because of the vital importance of their actions, each priest was highly trained and educated in their religion. But despite the knowledge, training, and explicit instructions, the priests were not translating what they were capable of into action.

That failure to act comes back to the idea that knowledge without application means nothing. I understand that's a strong statement. But remember how the priests interacted with knowledge—they didn't carry it on to completion. They knew everything they were supposed to know. They knew all about the Jewish tradition and the ritualistic behaviors. They knew the how, when, where, and why behind all of it. The priests were experts on religious practice and yet were still unfaithful in performing the sacrifices accurately.

Do you think American Christianity is more focused on knowing or doing? Why do you say that?

What sort of excuses might the priests have offered in their defense?

Think about it like this: What if I put you on the spot and asked you to share some of the information running around in your brain right now? What if I asked you to share a favorite song lyric or a popular line from a great movie? I bet you could do it. Your knowledge would translate into action. The same principle holds true for things like passwords and credit card numbers.

But what if it didn't? What if you stood in front of an ATM and couldn't get your fingers to key in the code that your brain was instructing them to type? This would be a problem, to say the least. Knowledge is empty if you can't apply it. That's really what was happening here with the priests. They knew exactly what they were supposed to be doing and

"Atonement will be made for you on this day to cleanse you, and you will be clean from all your sins before the LORD" (Leviticus 16:30).

During the Old Testament period, the tribe of Levi was responsible for the regulation of Israel's religious life. The tribe was divided into the priests and the rest of the Levites. The priests were the descendants of Aaron and held the primary responsibility for conducting worship. The rest of the Levites were the support staff who maintained the temple and conducted secondary religious duties.[14]

the spirit in which they should be doing it. However, their actions were far from the priestly standards God had established.

The priestly instructions aren't the only place the Bible describes this type of obedient lifestyle. Consider Luke 6:46-49 and the scary implications it holds:

"'Why do you call Me "Lord, Lord," and don't do the things I say? I will show you what someone is like who comes to Me, hears My words, and acts on them: He is like a man building a house, who dug deep and laid the foundation on the rock. When the flood came, the river crashed against that house and couldn't shake it, because it was well built. But the one who hears and does not act is like a man who built a house on the ground without a foundation. The river crashed against it, and immediately it collapsed. And the destruction of that house was great!'"

Or how about the harsh words James delivered in his book:

"But be doers of the word and not hearers only, deceiving yourselves. Because if anyone is a hearer of the word and not a doer, he is like a man looking at his own face in a mirror; for he looks at himself, goes away, and right away forgets what kind of man he was. But the one who looks intently into the perfect law of freedom and perseveres in it, and is not a forgetful hearer but a doer who acts—this person will be blessed in what he does" (James 1:22-25).

What is your immediate reaction to passages like these?

How do you square passages like this with grace? Do these passages promote salvation through works? Why or why not?

It's safe to say the Bible is clear on this point: God is not pleased with our inability to put motion to our understanding of His Word and His calling for our lives.

WHAT DO WE KNOW?

I was never very good with math in school, but I at least grasp the basic premise of some simple equations. For example, an addition problem

James was not one of the twelve disciples, nor did he believe in Jesus during Jesus' lifetime. He was converted by a resurrection appearance of Christ and took over the Jerusalem church after James the disciple was killed. He understood himself to be a missionary to the Jews, a counterpart to Paul, the missionary to the Gentiles.

might look as follows: 2 + 2 = 4. Or a multiplication equation might look something like: 3 x 3 = 9. It seems as if an "equation" of sorts can be found in the midst of Paul's writings—something along the lines of: belief + actions = pleasing God.

For us, it's important to not make the same mistake that the priests did regarding knowledge. In the New Testament, we see the apostle Paul teaching the same message. Paul used transitional language that challenged his readers to move from doctrine to duty, from principle to practice, and from belief to behavior.[15] His basic pattern was to introduce a theological truth and then provide instruction on how that principle is translated into one's daily life.

So in Galatians 5:1, the Bible says:

"It is for freedom that Christ has set us free. *Stand firm, then*, and do not let yourselves be burdened again by a yoke of slavery" (NIV, **emphasis added**).

Do you see it? The theological truth is that Christ has set us free. Applying that truth involves avoiding the trap of being burdened again by slavery.

Or consider the Book of Ephesians. Through three chapters, Paul expounded on the bigness of Christ in the universe and how God is busy bringing all things together under the head of Christ. His transition from knowledge to application comes in Ephesians 4:1:

"As a prisoner for the Lord, *then, I urge you* to live a life worthy of the calling you have received" (NIV, **emphasis added**).

The same thing is true in Philippians 2:1-2:

"If you have any encouragement from being united with Christ, if any comfort from his love, if any fellowship with the Spirit, if any tenderness and compassion, then make my joy complete by being like-minded, having the same love, being one in spirit and purpose."

In each case, Paul taught a spiritual principle, but he never left that principle as a matter strictly for knowledge. Each time he made sure his audience understood that the principle must be translated into everyday, practical action. And these are just a few examples. If you take your Bible and read several verses (or chapters), particularly in the writings of Paul, you'll quickly notice the intentionality of the apostle's

Another test case for Paul's methodology is the Book of Romans. He spent 11 chapters describing grace, faith, and sin, and it wasn't until chapter 12 that he wrote: "Therefore, brothers, by the mercies of God, I urge you to present your bodies as a living sacrifice, holy and pleasing to God; this is your spiritual act of worship."

writing—how he summarizes a large portion of doctrine into one clear statement before pushing his readers to application.

Over and over throughout Scripture, we see the need for our actions to line up with what we believe. Malachi was attempting to confront the empty religion of his day. This very same tenet of Malachi's message remained a continual instruction throughout the rest of the Bible.

In short, religion is empty without action.

Consider some of the things we know to be true:
- God created us each unique in the image of Himself.
- He has a plan for each of our lives.
- Through Christ we can be forgiven of our sins and redeemed from our past.
- God calls us to love Him and love people.
- We're called to serve and reach out to the lost, hurting, and needy.
- We're called to honor our father and mother.
- Jesus is the only way to God.
- Each individual is eternally separated from God without trusting his or her life to Christ.
- Heaven and hell are real places.
- The Holy Spirit is real and active in our lives.
- The Bible is the authoritative Word of God.

The list could go on and on. But the question remains—how do each of these things we know translate into daily life? Or do they at all?

Which three of the above facts about God most resonate with you?

What single thing do you think most prevents you from linking action to your spiritual knowledge?

A "creed" is a statement of belief recited as part of a religious service. From the Latin *credo*, for "I believe," creeds are succinct statements regarding the fundamentals of faith. Some of the most famous Christian creeds include the Nicene Creed and the Apostles' Creed.

JUST BECAUSE YOU CAN, DOESN'T MEAN YOU DO

Sometimes we look for any excuse to rationalize our spiritual apathy, don't we? What about our absence of prayer or discipline to His Word? Or what about not sharing the gospel with others? What about not tithing? As you thought through the list of things we know to be true above and reasoned through why you had a disconnect between your beliefs and your behaviors, I would imagine that several different theories came to mind. Some of these may have been quite valid, and I would imagine that some of them simply were not. In truth, I would imagine that some of them were nothing more than excuses, placing fault on other people, outside circumstances, or matters that are supposedly out of your control. But they are still excuses.

Which excuse is your favorite? How do you tend to justify your spiritual apathy?

For me personally, the "I would if I could" excuse seems to work well. I justify my inaction by claiming I would actually follow through on my knowledge if only my circumstances were different. It looks a little like this:

"I would give to the church if I was making enough to pay my bills first."
"I would be inviting people to church if I knew of a good one."
"I would be more active in serving if I didn't have so much going on."
"I would study the Bible daily if I didn't have to work overtime."
"I would have a better attitude if people were nicer."

It's easy to justify statements like these. Honestly, I can easily catch myself starting to feel sorry for the people who might be making them: *Just think about how stressed they must be or how tough their lives probably are.* Or, *How can you expect someone to obey God in the midst of a crazy schedule like that? Maybe they could be faithful in a few things, but it's unreasonable to think about them giving God their whole lives.*

Despite how easy it is to think this way, it simply doesn't validate the excuse. First, God certainly understands the challenges and obstacles in our lives, but we are still called to live in a way that brings honor and glory to Him. But secondly, the notion that our external circumstances excuse us from obedience is almost always invalid when we really begin to investigate the true nature of those situations. That was certainly true for the Levitical priests.

Listen to "The Tie That Binds" by Sandra McCracken on the *Blemished* playlist. Your leader will send you the whole playlist via e-mail, or you can find it at *threadsmedia.com/media.* Use these songs as the background music for your study.

Have you ever used external circumstances to justify your lack of obedience? What were the circumstances?

Why is it so easy to do that?

The priests had the responsibility of performing sacrificial offerings correctly by presenting God with pleasing and acceptable animal sacrifices. Instead, they presented defiled offerings—lame, crippled, and second-rate animals.

Look in Leviticus 22:17-33 and see all that was involved in whether an offering was acceptable or unacceptable. Here's just a sampling:

- The offering must be from the cattle, sheep, or goats (v. 19).
- The animal must not be blind, injured, maimed, or have a running sore, festering rash, or scabs (v. 22).
- It must not have an elongated or stunted limb (v. 23).
- It must not have bruised, crushed, torn, or severed testicles (v. 24).
- When an ox, sheep, or goat is born, it must remain with its mother for seven days; from the eighth day on, it will be acceptable as a gift (v. 27).

And the list goes on. Talk about a high standard! If anyone was justified in using the "I would if I could" excuse, it certainly would've been the Levitical priests. When you really begin to think about all that was involved in keeping the priests from presenting an acceptable offering, you can understand their potential challenges in doing so. Yet in Malachi, the nature of the rebuke implies that acceptable animals were available for sacrifice. Take a look at Malachi 1:7-8a,13:

"'You place defiled food on my altar. But you ask, 'How have we defiled you?' By saying that the LORD's table is contemptible. When you bring blind animals for sacrifice, is that not wrong . . . You bring stolen, lame, or sick animals. You bring this as an offering! Am I to accept that from your hands?' asks the LORD" (NIV).

R

Allen Ross writes extensively concerning the nature of sacrifices and the theological implications in Leviticus in his helpful commentary *Holiness to the Lord.*

If God was angered at the Levitical priests presenting blemished offerings, one can conclude that they also had the choice of an unblemished offering. And, if choice exists, then so does ability.

This is not just an instance where the priests simply didn't have anything else to offer to God. In others words, they couldn't use the "I would present God an acceptable offering if I simply had one" excuse. It says in Malachi 1:14:

"'The deceiver is cursed who has an acceptable male in his flock and makes a vow but sacrifices a defective animal to the Lord. For I am a great King,' says the Lord of Hosts, 'and My name will be feared among the nations.'"

It appears the Levitical priests had all they needed to please God. Their obedience to God was not a matter of ability but rather a matter of willingness.

The natural question for us then is this: "What's my excuse?" If anyone had obstacles to pleasing God, the priests with their strict rules and regulations did. Today, we also are given incredible opportunities and abilities to present before God. And yet, we often use our supposed inabilities as our greatest excuses. This is unacceptable and unpleasing to God. We've been given all that we need and more to serve Him, but we often don't take advantage of it.

The list is long, but here are a few of the great gifts we've been given:
- The Bible
- The Holy Spirit
- Freedom to worship
- The Church

What are some of the others you would add?

Listen to "Connecting with Malachi—Part I" as author Jason Hayes discusses some additional implications from the Book of Malachi. Your group leader will send it to you via e-mail.

The priests had knowledge and ability yet often missed the mark on serving the Father. In the same way, we are granted knowledge, abilities, and much more. Let's not be like the priests. May our knowledge, abilities, and other blessings lead to application.

REFLECTING ON MALACHI

Continue reading through the Book of Malachi, focusing on Malachi 1:6–2:9. Spend some time reflecting on the following questions:

☆ **How had the nation's leadership failed during the days of Malachi?**

☆ **What principles of leadership can you glean from these verses?**

☆ **Who are people you have influence over? How are you using that influence?**

☆ **What other implications does this passage have for people outside the clergy?**

In conjunction with your reading in Malachi, spend some time reading Romans 2. Focus particularly on verses 17-24.

☆ **What phrases stand out to you in this passage?**

☆ **What similarities do you see to Malachi?**

3 WARPED MOTIVES

THE DISCONNECT BETWEEN "WHAT" AND "WHY"

THE HIGH PRIEST HAD A HUGE BURDEN ON HIS SHOULDERS THAT DAY. As he walked slowly from the outer court into the internal one, he must have felt the weight. It was the weight of sin, not just the sin of the people, but the reminder that he himself was one of the people, and some of the weight he bore was from his own sins.

Before he could make a sacrifice on behalf of the people, he must first make a sacrifice on his own behalf. That's what the blood of the bull was for, because he was a sinner too. Even the high priest had to recognize his shortcomings, for he must know that regardless of how much good he did, evil was crouched right next to him. Even his most gracious actions and best works must be cleansed with blood. His actions were tainted by the impurity of motive. And walking into the innermost room, into the presence of the holy, he must have remembered the countless times his heart was impure.

YOU WOULDN'T DARE …

I had a series of jobs throughout high school and college that were, well … diverse. Take my first job, for example—a brief stint at a place called Celebration Station. Imagine a Chuck E. Cheese on steroids, and you've got Celebration Station. It had go-karts, bumper boats, putt-putt, video games, and all the other stuff that comes along with being a mecca for over-stimulated kids. Here, in this casino for kindergartners, I was Harry the Hound Dog.

The big, plush, lovable dog would make appearances for birthday parties and special events. Although the costume was outlandishly hot, I tried to remain focused on my responsibilities—to entertain people and help them have a great time. And let me tell you, I earned my money in that suit. I worked hard. Really hard. I tried to go the extra mile, even if it meant riding in an enormous dog suit alongside an uncoordinated 8-year-old in a speeding go-kart. Delightful, huh? Ultimately, I was working hard because I had a boss who I desired to please. I knew that the security and success of my job was closely connected to my ability to satisfy the expectations he had set forth. And I wanted to give my best in order to meet those expectations.

Another job that I had was with Nabisco. I was the cookie man. As the cookie man, I served as a temp for full-time employees while they took their vacations throughout the summer. These employees had a territory of stores they were responsible for, and each store had a huge inventory of Nabisco products. The Nabisco employees were to keep stores updated with fresh products, new displays, and more.

My job was to do for one week in their territory what they did all the remaining weeks of the year. And though I was paid very well for a summer job, I had no idea what I was getting myself into. I went into it thinking that I was going to have a blast and eat lots of cookies and crackers, but I was wrong. Instead, I quickly found out that I couldn't stock shelves fast enough or move through inventory quick enough. Each day, I worked as hard as I possibly could and yet still struggled to complete my assignments. That stressed me out, but not because of my passion for Oreos®. I got so wound up because I wanted to do a good job for my boss and the people I was filling in for.

Then there was the time I spent on the "caf staff" during my freshman year of college, doing everything from unloading the freezer trucks each day as they brought supplies, to helping with the dishes, to preparing certain foods, to wiping down tables. I liked to think of myself as a culinary Renaissance man. I remember one morning when

Listen to "Connecting with Malachi—Part II" as author Jason Hayes discusses some additional implications from the Book of Malachi. Your group leader will send it to you via e-mail.

I accidentally filled the huge sweet tea pots with salt as opposed to sugar. Hey, they are both white and grainy, right?

I was mortified in thinking about how my classmates would respond. I hurriedly made new pots and replaced the bad tea with the correct mix. If they had ordered tea, that's what I wanted them to have. I was determined to please the customer.

The common theme throughout my odd jobs focuses on motivation, or specifically, the priority of pleasing someone else. Whether a boss, a colleague, a customer, or a classmate, I felt the responsibility to do my job to the best of my ability. But, even more, I didn't want to let anyone down. And while the principles of hard work and commitment I learned during those years are very valuable, my motivation raises some interesting questions that relate back to Malachi's rebuke toward the Levitical priests and the people of Israel.

> **How much value do you place in keeping the commitments that you've made to other people?**

Listen to "Learning How to Die" by Jon Foreman on the *Blemished* playlist. Your leader will send you the whole playlist via e-mail, or you can find it at *threadsmedia.com/media*. Use these songs as the background music for your study.

> **How much time and energy do you spend trying to please other people in your life?**

> **Are those things wrong? At what point do they become wrong?**

Those questions become even more stark when we weigh them against another set of more important questions:

> **Do you invest more in pleasing men than pleasing God? Why or why not?**

Do you interact with God in ways that you wouldn't with other people? Why or why not?

Do you worry about the things of your humanity more than the things of divinity? Why or why not?

We wouldn't dare treat people how we often treat God. That's what the priests were doing, and that's what we do, too.

WHO'S YOUR GOVERNOR?
Read Malachi 1:8. What is God's point in this verse?

How can you personalize that question?

Malachi 1:8 uses a Hebrew idiom which is literally translated "raise the face." The phrase "indicates acceptance and a positive response," and God's point was that such a weak sacrifice would not even raise the face of the local governor, much less the God of the universe.[16]

As we've seen in previous sessions, Malachi gave a lot of attention to how the Levitical priests presented their offerings before God. We see that issue again in Malachi 1:8:

"'Bring it to your governor! Would he be pleased with you or show you favor? [Would he accept you?]' asks the LORD of Hosts."

So Malachi was not only challenging the Levitical priests about issues of action and ability, but he was also addressing things like priorities and motive.

How does a verse about a governor relate back to the topic of priorities and motive? Well, I would suggest that in most cases what we do best illustrates our priorities. For example, it's hard to believe someone who claims to be passionate about the environment but drives a gas-guzzling vehicle, doesn't recycle, and never turns off their lights. The action gives validity to the claim.

In the case of the priests, I'm sure they would've claimed that their hearts were pure and priorities were straight. After all, their whole lives were built around their priestly duties. If serving in that capacity wasn't number one on their motive list, then they were in the wrong line of work. And yet their actions told a different story: "The priests had the audacity to offer God what their governor, as a form of taxation, would never have accepted from them. They were more fearful of the governor's rejection than of God's. This would have been during the time that Nehemiah was back in Persia (cf. Nehemiah 3:6) when he would have relinquished the office for some time."[17]

It seems obvious to say, but the governor only ruled over temporal things. God governs over all of creation. How could the priests have missed this? But before we judge too quickly, maybe we should ask the same thing of ourselves. Are we missing it, too?

Our level of priority reveals very much about what we believe about God. We can make grand claims about how much we value God, respect His authority, and desire to live for Him, but until we start *prioritizing* Him, we haven't really internalized those things. The truth is that we are far more committed to other areas of life than we are to God.

What does it mean to "prioritize" God?

Where does God rank on your own list? How do you know?

Take a moment and think about all that you're involved in and all that encompasses your commitments and responsibilities. Take a moment and think about how you approach those matters. Now think clearly about how you approach matters that relate to God. Do your standards line up? Does your work ethic and commitment reveal His greatness and authority? What kind of priorities do your actions reveal? And if they seem to imply something different than what you are comfortable with, what does that mean?

We all too often spend our lives trying to please an employer or a boss. Others try to please their friends or family. Still others try to please the

One of the most accurate gauges of our priorities is our pocketbook. According to *Passing the Plate: Why American Christians Don't Give Away More Money*, 20 percent of U.S. Christians give no money to their church. The book continues, "If American Christians could somehow find a way to move to practices of reasonably generous giving, they could generate, over above what they currently give, a total of another $133.4 billion a year to devote to whatever purposes and needs they would choose."[18]

world by committing themselves to social action. None of these things are bad ideas. In fact, God is honored in these kinds of commitments. But He ceases to be honored when those commitments take a greater priority than our commitment to please Him. We must first commit to a constant pursuit to please God, and we must do so with such intensity that those efforts dwarf any efforts we might make toward other things.

I would imagine that you give significant time and attention to your school commitments. I would guess that you don't make a habit of being defiant toward your boss. I would think that you respect and follow the guidelines of the organizations that you are a part of. I would say the same things about myself. So why is it that we catch ourselves cheating God in ways we would never think about in other areas of our lives? God was calling the priests out on this matter. And, in a sense, He's doing the same thing to us now.

I'd encourage you to take a few moments and ask yourself about the "why" behind all of this. Don't go any further until you really wrestle through this in a time of personal investigation.

According to the United States Department of Labor (*dol.gov*), in 200 7 about 25 percent of Americans spent time volunteering through or for an organization. Persons in their early 20s were the least likely to volunteer.

What are some reasons we tend to lose track of what's really important?

What are some practical ways to keep those things of greatest importance in their proper place?

THE "WHY" BEHIND IT ALL

I hope that you are beginning to see that the idea behind *Blemished* isn't just about the actual physical offering that we present before God. What we see modeled in Malachi is a disconnect between the actions of the priests and their supposed convictions. And one can only conclude that if such a disconnect exists, then possibly their supposed convictions aren't quite as "convicting" as they might like people to believe. The next question that naturally arises is this, "Why would I follow the commands of God if my heart wasn't connected to a genuine and authentic relationship with Him?"

It's not like following God makes you rich, famous, powerful, or prestigious. In fact, quite the opposite has proven to be true throughout history. The Christian life is difficult and Christianity is demanding. It's not like you are getting a guaranteed hot date and tickets to Disney World. The Christian walk requires sacrifice and commitment. It affects your thoughts about money, sex, relationships, career, and so much more. So the question still remains—why would anyone model their life around so-called "Christian" values if their heart seems disconnected to these matters?

What we're seeing in Malachi's rebuke is that the priests were guilty of both errors in practice and impurity in heart. These things go together; in fact, they are impossible to separate. The priests weren't the only ones in faith history who substituted "action" for "heart." The Pharisees during the days of Jesus did the same things. They were busy doing all kinds of things for God, performing their duties, all the while their hearts were far from God's true intent. And Jesus' reaction? It was the harshest criticism imaginable. Calling them broods of vipers, whitewashed tombs, and dirtied cups, Jesus pointed out that bad actions come from bad hearts.

What is a modern paraphrase of Jesus' above criticism of the Pharisees?

In those terms, what might Jesus say to 21st century Christ followers?

In other words, it's pretty tough to live for Christ when your heart is apathetic to things of God. It's amazing we often still try to pull it off. I'm sure we could all list several examples of when our hearts haven't lined up with our lifestyle in the past.

Take a moment and think of some reasons why one might continue to try to do the "right thing" while remaining complacent toward God in his or her heart. I'll help get you started with some examples and also what these individuals might be thinking.

In a culture that so highly values tolerance, it's somewhat ironic that the number of martyrs for the Christian faith in the 20th century far exceeded any previous century. Though the numbers cannot be accurately calculated, you can visit *persecution.com* for some of their stories.

For the specific charges against the Pharisees, read Matthew 23 and reflect on Jesus' strong point to the religious leaders of His day.

- Family heritage. (They've always done it this way, so it doesn't matter if I really connect with it or not.)
- Social pressures. (It's easier to go with the current than against it.)
- Blind hope. (If I live like this, good things might happen to me.)

Do any of the above reasons resonate with you? Which one(s)? Why?

What would you add to the list?

I'm sure you came up with a number of other possibilities, but I think it's important that we focus in on one in particular—the idea of motives.

Previously, we looked at Malachi 1:14, but I want us to examine it briefly from a new perspective. It says:

"'The deceiver is cursed who has an acceptable male in his flock and makes a vow but sacrifices a defective animal to the Lord. For I am a great King,' says the Lord of Hosts, 'and My name will be feared among the nations.'"

We already talked about the priests' refusal to align their actions with their abilities; that is, even though they had the ability to offer a right sacrifice they chose not to do so. What we didn't discuss was how they actually went about shortchanging God. Let's examine what really happened here.

Remember that the Scripture was clear. The law required the priest to present an unblemished, male animal. Such an animal was considered of great value, and was meant to be brought with sincerity and joy. That's what the Levitical priests publicly said they would do during the days of Malachi. But at the last minute, they would substitute a blemished female. And that switch happened in secret.[19]

What does the secretive nature reveal about motive?

In Malachi 1:13, Malachi used three words to describe the sacrifices: "crippled," "diseased," and "injured." The third word comes from a verb meaning "to steal, pilfer, take by clandestine means." Other uses of this word can be found in Leviticus 19:3; Judges 9:25; and Job 24:2.

The priests publicly vowed to give God their best and then did not privately follow through. Secrecy is a huge indicator of wrong motives. Evidently, the priests were more interested in people seeing them serve God than actually serving God, and there is a world of difference between the two. Sometimes people have an empty relationship with God because of insincere motives. They are more interested in the benefits of being associated with godly things than actually living for Him. This raises an important question for us to think about: Are we interested in impressing people or impressing God? They are two very different things.

First Peter 1:13-16 reminds us:

"Therefore, get your minds ready for action, being self-disciplined, and set your hope completely on the grace to be brought to you at the revelation of Jesus Christ. As obedient children, do not be conformed to the desires of your former ignorance but, as the One who called you is holy … for it is written, Be holy, because I am holy."

We are called to be holy because God is holy, not because other people are watching and holiness looks good on our spiritual résumés. We should be holy because God deserves it. Man, that's a great truth for us!

In Acts 5, Ananias was guilty of something similar to what the priests were doing. We read:

"But a man named Ananias, with Sapphira his wife, sold a piece of property. However, he kept back part of the proceeds with his wife's knowledge, and brought a portion of it and laid it at the apostles' feet. Then Peter said, 'Ananias, why has Satan filled your heart to lie to the Holy Spirit and keep back part of the proceeds from the field? Wasn't it yours while you possessed it? And after it was sold, wasn't it at your disposal? Why is it that you planned this thing in your heart? You have not lied to men but to God!'" (Acts 5:1-4).

We may be capable of deceiving a lot of people around us. They may look at us and even admire what we present publicly despite our private shortcomings. We may deceive other people. But we will never deceive God. First Corinthians 4:5 says:

"He will bring to light what is hidden in darkness and will expose the motives of men's hearts. At that time each will receive his praise from God" (NIV).

First Peter was a letter directed to suffering believers. It was written by Peter from Rome to persecuted Christians in northwest and central portions of present day Turkey. The situation there was probably one in which Christians were seen as a threat to the social structure because of their refusal to sacrifice to the emperor. This charge was enough to incite social ostracism and mob violence in communities against Christians.

The sad end to the story of Ananias and Sapphira in Acts 5 is that both were struck dead on the spot because of their dishonesty.

When you meet with your small group this week, watch "Why Worry?," a video short found on the *Blemished* leader kit. Think about what could be accomplished if we all brought our unblemished sacrifices together.

According to the United States Department of Agriculture, American households throw away approximately 470 pounds of food each year.

We also see in Proverbs 16:2-5:

"All a man's ways seem right in his own eyes, but the LORD weighs the motives. Commit your activities to the LORD and your plans will be achieved. The LORD has prepared everything for His purpose—even the wicked for the day of disaster. Everyone with a proud heart is detestable to the LORD; be assured, he will not go unpunished."

At the end of the day, we must be reminded of our goal. Our prayer needs to be that people won't look at our lives and think what great people we are. Instead, we should be praying that people look at our lives and think what a great God we serve! We must not slip into the trap of serving God to please men.

Take some time and think about a few of your actions. Are there ever times when you do those things simply to appease or impress people, not because your heart is connected to them? Here are a few things to consider:

- Attending church
- Serving others
- Praying in public

After adding some of your own thoughts to this list, spend a few moments asking God to help you avoid this element of empty religion in the future.

YOU'RE GOING TO GIVE IT TO WHOM?

I never really cared for leftovers. I don't want to come across snobby or wasteful. Rather, I think I just really like things that are fresh. I like fresh pizza and fresh fruit. I can think of very few dishes that are as good the second time around as they were the first. I definitely can't think of anything that is actually better the third time around than when it was first served. Don't get me wrong. I still eat them. I just prefer fresh.

Imagine for a moment being invited to a really special meal for your birthday. Your friends hosted a dinner and they all came to celebrate your life and your friendship. Despite their promises of a feast, they actually all decided to just empty their respective fridges and compile a bunch of leftovers. Wow—what a let down! You came expecting filet mignon and instead found Sally's chicken fingers from Thursday and Tim's moldy salad from last week. Doesn't seem like much of a celebration, does it? As you consider your relationship with the Lord and your life in the context of being an offering unto Him, are you presenting to Him your best or your leftovers? Your life should be a celebration of His greatness and appreciation for the relationship you can have with Him through the work of Jesus. I don't like leftovers and as we learned in Malachi, neither does God. I hope as you've explored the ideas of priority and motive, you are gaining a better understanding of what an "unblemished offering" looks like today.

In what sense are we guilty of offering our leftovers?

A few years ago, I read a story on the Internet that was attributed back to the famous radio personality, Paul Harvey. According to the site, Harvey told the following story that I believe makes a poignant statement. The story is as follows:

The Butterball company set up a Thanksgiving hotline to answer questions about cooking turkeys. One woman asked if she could use a turkey that had been in the bottom of her freezer for … 23 years. The Butterball expert (how's that for a job title?) told her it would probably be safe if the freezer had been below zero the entire time. But the expert warned her that even if the turkey was safe to eat, the flavor would likely have deteriorated and wouldn't be worth eating. The woman said, "That's what I thought. We'll give the turkey to our church." [20]

Although we'll spend an upcoming session discussing our interactions with the local church, the recipient of this person's "generosity" is not the point. The point for me is the visible expression of her misplaced priorities and poor motives. She wouldn't dare serve that to anyone else, but was more than willing to present it to God (through the church). In addition, why was she giving? There is only one option. It certainly wasn't for the enjoyment of others or out of service to God. Rather, it was for the viewing and approval of man. Obviously, this was a ridiculous response. But let us be slow to judge. We need to be evaluating our own life in these matters constantly. God doesn't want our leftovers; nor does He want our second-rate offerings. May what we've been processing thus far and what we'll be learning ahead get us closer to honoring Him in all facets of our life.

Generousgiving.org reveals that the average amount of money given by a full or confirmed member of a U.S. Christian church in 2004 was $691.93. This comes to an average of $13.31 per week.

REFLECTING ON MALACHI

Continue reading through the Book of Malachi, focusing on Malachi 2:10-16. Spend some time reflecting on the following issues:

✦ **What is significant about the manner of the sacrifices that were being presented?**

✦ **Why does God care so much about marriage?**

✦ **Does His attitude toward marriage have any implications for those who aren't married?**

✦ **How does it make you feel to see God use the word "hate"?**

In conjunction with your reading in Malachi, spend some time reading Ephesians 5. Focus particularly on verses 22-33.

✦ **What phrases stand out to you in this passage?**

✦ **What similarities do you see to Malachi?**

4 LAME ATTITUDES

THE DISPARITY BETWEEN "WHAT" AND "HOW"

THERE WAS CERTAINLY NO ROOM FOR FLIPPANCY IN THE ACTIONS OF THE PRIEST. He had to be careful because the manner in which he offered the sacrifice was as important as the sacrifice itself. His attitude was of great consequence. He couldn't just splatter blood around as if the sacrifice was something merely to get through; every part of the process had to be done with care.

The people waiting in the courtyard felt the somberness and expectancy of the day, too. Idle conversations and wandering thoughts were things for another day. Their attitude reflected a sense of humility, repentance, and hopefulness for the mercy of God. So they waited, holding their breaths, focused on what they could only imagine was taking place behind the curtain.

WHERE WE'VE BEEN AND WHERE WE'RE GOING

I've often heard it said, "It's not always just about what you do, but also about how you do it." That feels appropriate in the context of Malachi. Remember what has led us to this point in our study of Malachi's rebuke of the Levitical priests and the people of Israel:

- We've studied the background of all that was happening around Malachi's prophetic message, including the divine silence that followed it.
- We've developed the "blemished" idea as it relates to the sacrificial system of the past and its parallels to our walk with God today.
- We've established that while we are already a fragrant and perfect offering before God because of the redeeming work of Jesus, we are still called to obedience in our daily lives.
- While studying Malachi's ancient rebuke, we've examined our own lives and asked ourselves some tough questions related to our actions, abilities, priorities, and motives.

What part of the study so far has been most meaningful to you?

How has your life changed since beginning the study?

A *motive* is "something that causes a person to act in a certain way." An *attitude* is "the manner, disposition, or feeling with regard to a person or thing, especially in the mind."

Our motives in our relationship with God have an incredible amount to do with our offerings, but so do our attitudes and energy. Those elements themselves can determine whether or not an offering is "blemished" or "unblemished" sacrifice before the Lord. Granted, motives and attitude run pretty close together, but there is a key difference between them. A motive is the ultimate reason behind what you do or don't do; an attitude involves the actual act itself. How do you bring your sacrifice to the Lord? Is it gratefully and thankfully? Or is it reluctantly and bitterly? An attitude, whether right or wrong, can make all the difference.

How would you describe your own attitude in bringing offerings to the Lord?

What sorts of things influence your attitude, either positively or negatively?

"Be careful not to practice your righteousness in front of people, to be seen by them. Otherwise, you will have no reward from your Father in heaven" (Matthew 6:1).

For me personally, I struggle much more with doing things for the right reason and with the right spirit rather than just doing them in general. I'm willing to do what I deem the Lord requires of me, but often that's why I do it—because He requires it. The Levitical priests and the people of Israel struggled with the same thing. And so all of us come, sometimes with the right sacrifice, but often with frowns on our faces and resentment in our hearts.

In addition to examining our attitudes, it's important that we also take stock of our energy and how we should be using it best to honor God. Again, this is much easier to think about as a generic principle instead of actually applying it to the minutia of our lives. But we have to move beyond theory to action. Our goal is to honor God with our entire being—body, soul, and spirit. That can't happen if we avoid wrestling through such difficult topics.

Do you think God cares more about the act or the attitude and motive behind the act? What makes you say that?

WE'RE NOT FINISHED YET

"We're not finished yet." Those aren't really comforting words at times. Have you ever found yourself in a situation where words like that caused you to cringe? Maybe you've heard these words during a busy shift at work. Or maybe from a professor in school. Maybe it was from a coach or personal trainer. Maybe "we're not finished yet" brings back horrific memories of chores from your childhood.

Although I think I've heard that phrase muttered in each of those settings, I'm not sure any instance will ever be as poignant as when I heard it in my first half marathon. I'm not sure what made me want to run 13.1 miles, but there I was, a rookie to the world of endurance racing, beginning a near sprint toward what I thought was the finish line. That's when the horror set in.

The marathon—a 26.2 mile race—has its origins in the legend of the run of the soldier Pheidippides from a battlefield at the site of the town of Marathon, Greece, to Athens in 490 B.C. It's said that Pheidippides delivered the message of victory, then collapsed and died.

For a different take on what the Christian life is supposed to look like, check out *Metamorpha: Jesus as a Way of Life* by Kyle Strobel.

Pastor and author Francis Chan expands on what a relationship with Christ built on love really looks like. Check out his book *Crazy Love*.

I had somehow gotten caught up in the craziness of the race and lost track of the mileage. I was sure I was within a few hundred yards of finishing, so I was shocked to see the sign on the course telling me I had one more mile to go. In my anguish, I must have verbalized my confusion to the runners around me. It was at that point that I heard the cursed phrase, "We're not finished yet, buddy!" What made it worse was that it came from a guy maybe twice my age running next to me. Not good. I was exhausted and angered at my own confusion.

We must be cautious of falling into the trap of inaccurately deeming ourselves as spiritually complete, when in actuality we still have much further to go. Lots of people live their entire Christian lives this way. They live like Christianity is a mountain climb, and every so often they get to a flat place to camp and look around at where they came from as if to say, "I'm doing pretty good. Look how far I've come." If you live life with that attitude, the inevitable result is spiritual pride and laziness, and contentment with your level of intimacy with the Lord.

Have you ever met someone who was convinced he or she had "arrived"? What did you think of that person?

Does God ever intend for us to "arrive"? Why or why not?

How does your answer above influence your attitude?

It's remarkably easy for us to work through the spiritual inventory of our lives, checking off all the disciplines we may be actively participating in and naturally considering ourselves to be "holy." We examine our list and see things such as attending church, tithing, reading Scripture, serving others, and more. But what we see in Malachi is a challenge to live differently than that. It's not a challenge to live life on the mountaintop, but on the path, walking with Jesus, knowing that the goal isn't about reaching a certain level but about an honest and loving relationship with Him.

Re-read Malachi 2:1-9. Then read 2:10-17 and 3:6-18. How do you see these passages fitting together?

In the passage above, Malachi was challenging the priests (1:6–2:9) and the people (2:10-16) to more than just the physicality of their faith. According to the prophet, their spirituality isn't just about completing a certain set of instructions. It's more. It's deeper. He's challenging them to evaluate inward matters, to ask the hard questions of "why" and "how" that accompany their physical acts of sacrifice.

Although we've discussed much about the sacrificial system and the idea of offerings in our past sessions, these weren't the only accusations Malachi made. The people were also guilty of marrying foreign wives (2:10-12) and divorcing the wives of their youth (2:13-16). Interestingly enough, long before Malachi came on the scene, Nehemiah addressed many of the same issues. The people of his day violated the Sabbath. They abused their priestly office. And they abandoned their Jewish wives in favor of marrying women from the surrounding nations (cf. Nehemiah 13).[21] But there's something else, something deeper, that Malachi confronted more frequently than anything else—attitude.

Do you tend to think more often about your attitude or your physical actions of obedience? Why?

There is little question as to God's opinion about all of these matters. He said some pretty shocking stuff to the priests in Malachi 2:3:

"Because of you I will rebuke your descendants; I will spread on your faces the offal from your festival sacrifices, and you will be carried off with it" (NIV).

Ouch. That's certainly not something I'm comfortable hearing from God. Normally, the animal waste of the sacrificial system was carried outside the camp to be burned, so to hear the Lord of the universe say He will smear dung on my face is a pretty good indication of His disapproval (Exodus 29:14; Leviticus 4:11-12, 8:17, 16:27). Just as that

When God sent Israel into the promised land to conquer it, He gave the people strict guidelines about intermarriage. He knew that integrating the lifestyles and customs of the conquered peoples would be detrimental to His people's identity as those set apart for Himself, so He urged them to not marry foreign wives.

The word translated *offal* is literally dung, or the undigested food remaining in the stomach of a sacrificed animal.[22]

waste was meant to be immediately and properly disposed of, so the Lord was willing to humiliate and toss out the priests.

But something else stands out in these verses. Malachi 2:1-3 describes unfaithfulness as something bigger and deeper than simple, physical actions. Instead, it's getting at this "we're not done yet" notion. God is saying that heart matters are as crucial, if not more so, as any other matter when it comes to pleasing Him. It seems that "being faithful" is more than accomplishing the things on the Christian checklist. Malachi proclaims, "'Therefore, this decree is for you priests: If you don't listen, and if you don't take it to heart to honor My name,' says the LORD of Hosts, 'I will send a curse among you . . .'" (2:1-2). The NKJV puts it like this: "If you will not hear, and if you will not take it to heart . . ." No matter the translation, the matter of one's heart is fundamental to the passage's meaning.

What do you think the Bible means when it talks about "the heart"?

Why are matters like these of such vital importance to God?

What does that importance reveal about the nature of God?

God continued to make His point in Malachi 2:4-6 as He reminded the priests and people of the relationship agreement that He set forth in the Levitical covenant. (Once again, the terms of that relationship can be seen in Numbers 3:44-48, 18:8-24; and Deuteronomy 33:8-11.) God specifically chose to remind them of the covenant He made with Aaron (of Levi's line) and his descendents. But there was a big difference between Aaron and the priests being addressed in Malachi, because "Aaron, unlike the priests of Malachi's time, feared and reverenced God."[24]

When the Bible refers to the heart, it means the seat and center of all physical and spiritual life. The soul, on the other hand, refers to the seat of thoughts, passions, desires, and affections.[23]

The Scripture says:

"My covenant with him was one of life and peace, and I gave these to him; it called for reverence, and he revered Me and stood in awe of My name" (Malachi 2:5).

What does the description of Aaron have to do with attitude?

Aaron was Moses' older brother. When Moses argued with God about his ability to go to Pharaoh on God's behalf, God appointed Aaron to be Moses' spokesperson. He was consistently associated with Moses in the great acts of Exodus and became the first high priest. But he also had a tendency toward disobedience, as in the instance when he led the people in creating the golden calf (Exodus 32).

Did you see the nature of God's demands? It wasn't simply a matter of physical requirement. What made Aaron different and special was Aaron's attitude toward God while performing his duties.

Attitude matters. A lot. It mattered to Malachi. It matters to God. But often it matters to us about as much as it mattered to the checklist-driven priests and people of Israel. Like them, we have a "just get it done" mentality when it comes to the things of God.

Why does an attitude like that dishonor God?

THE NATURE OF THEIR ATTITUDE

Throughout the entire book of Malachi, we see a constant banter between God and the priests. These exchanges reveal the condition of their hearts, which led to their disgraceful actions. In turn we also get a glimpse into their attitudes.

In His dialogue with the Levitical priests throughout Malachi, God was identifying the condition of the priests' attitude, all the while affirming His own character. Here are a few of the more poignant examples of the banter between God and the priests:

- Malachi 1:6-8
- Malachi 1:12-13
- Malachi 2:13-14
- Malachi 2:17
- Malachi 3:7-9
- Malachi 3:13-15

Read these passages in Malachi carefully, looking closely at the attitude, motive, and spirit of the priests. Then take some time and journal your response.

After looking over these passages, you probably began to see a pattern of attitude flaws revealed by the priests. And if you're like me, most of these flaws start to hit home. If we were completely honest in our conversations with God, we'd surely see many of these same attitudes rise to the surface.

> **Based on the passages above, how would you describe the attitude of the priests?**

> **Which of those verse are the most personally applicable to you?**

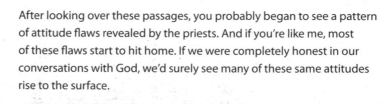

Listen to "Desperate Man" by Andy Gullahorn on the *Blemished* playlist. Your leader will send you the whole playlist via e-mail, or you can find it online at *threadsmedia.com/media*. Use these songs as the background music for your study.

At the end of Malachi 1:6, the Scripture says:

"It is you, O priests, who show contempt for my name. But you ask, 'How have we shown contempt for your name?'" (NIV).

The Lord was specific and pointed in His response, essentially saying, "You are showing contempt for My name by not doing anything like I asked, all while having a terrible attitude about it, you morons." Although He certainly was more God-like (He's good at that) in His response, that paraphrase isn't far from His point.

Even the priests' questions drip with their contempt. *Who does God, not to mention this prophet, think He is to bring such accusations against us? Doesn't He realize what we have given up? Doesn't He realize the commitment level He's asking for? We're doing His stupid sacrifices; can't anything ever satisfy Him?* Knowing what we do about the priests, their training, and their knowledge, we're left with just one real conclusion to this question. We know the priests weren't stupid and we know they weren't misinformed, so why do they even have to ask for specific examples? It seems they were in denial of their spiritual condition and had become calloused and apathetic toward the things of God.

Can you identify with the objections of the priests? Has there ever been a time when you've felt that way?

That's not a good conclusion. But it really seems that this is the only reason they would ask such questions. The same rationale holds true for the other questions that they were asking. They had entered into a delusional state and refused to recognize the truth of their actions and the reality of the heart condition that precipitated it. Such a denial of the truth, all the while continuing to offer these half-hearted attempts at religion, really made a mockery of God and His covenant. They were treating His love and faithfulness with contempt. That's not good either.

Look at Galatians 6:7-8:

"Don't be deceived: God is not mocked. For whatever a man sows he will also reap, because the one who sows to his flesh will reap corruption from the flesh, but the one who sows to the Spirit will reap eternal life from the Spirit."

So what do we take from this? And where do we go from here? First of all, we must recognize that there were times when the priests did exactly what was physically asked of them and yet still were not pleasing God. For example, look in Malachi 2:13:

"You cover the LORD's altar with tears, with weeping and groaning, because He no longer respects your offerings or receives them gladly from your hands."

In other words, there is a clear distinction in God's mind between simply doing something and doing it with a pure heart and a contrite spirit. I believe that is precisely what we should take away from this aspect of Malachi's rebuke.

What does "a pure heart and a contrite spirit" mean to you?

Paul wrote to the churches of the Galatian region in order to help them return to the true gospel. The church was splintered due to the influence of the Judaizers, a group of teachers claiming a person had to first become a Jew in order to become a Christian.

What are some steps you can take toward that attitude?

Chariots of Fire is the story of Eric Liddell, an Olympic athlete who saw his life as an offering to God. Take some time to view this movie that one the Academy Award for Best Picture in 1981.

In the last session, we discussed how our motives affect the "why" behind our actions. The challenge for this session is to evaluate the attitudes that often accompany those actions. In short, you need to be asking God daily to help your heart line up with your actions as you carry out those actions.

Wait a minute, you might say. *Isn't there something else? Isn't there something more I should do, a procedure of sorts I can run through to make sure I'm doing the right thing for the right reason in the right spirit?* Frankly, a procedure like that may create more harm than good. Procedures are what got the priests into this mess in the first place. No, we don't need more procedures; we need more humility. We need more honesty. We need more accurate assessments of our spiritual condition.

Oftentimes the simple act of recognizing that your attitude isn't right goes a long way to fixing it. Admitting that fallacy to God is in itself an act of humility, and an act that stands diametrically opposed to the defiant rebuttal questions of the priests. When we are willing to acknowledge to God the shortcomings in our own attitudes, then He will be faithful, over time, to develop the right heart in us. We remain humble, He remains active, and we remain in active relationship with each other.

I often pray in times of corporate worship that the words from my mouth would accurately reflect the condition of my heart. It seems appropriate to be striving to be consistent in all aspects of our lives. Take some time to really think about your attitude in general, and more specifically its impact on your connection to your "spiritual actions." Do you have some issues that you need to present to God related to any of the following?
- Anger
- Greed
- Jealousy
- Resentment
- Frustration
- Disappointment

What would you add to the list above?

Which of the issues relate most directly to you at this point in your life? Why?

Now think about your attitude, and whether or not we saw that same attitude played out in the lives of the Levitical priests. Is there a possibility that you too are actively involved in God-related actions while simultaneously having impure or negative attitudes? It's definitely something to consider. And be cautious. As rudimentary as this may seem, it's essential that we remember to keep God in the center of our evaluation process. We can't just try to correct our attitudes on our own, without His input and power.

When separated from the guiding work of the Holy Spirit and the truth of God's Word, we are always susceptible to deceiving ourselves about our own spiritual well-being. In a sense, that's what happened to the Levitical priests—they distorted their communion with Him and disobeyed the law they had committed to following. If you don't ever think about the need for spiritual development or improvement in your own life, then most likely you are in major need of it.

WHAT BURDEN?
"But you are profaning it when you say: 'The Lord's table is defiled, and its product, its food, is contemptible.' You also say: 'Look what a nuisance!' 'And you scorn it,' says the LORD of hosts. 'You bring stolen, lame, or sick animals. You bring this as an offering! Am I to accept that from your hands?' asks the LORD" (Malachi 1:12-13).

The Levitical priests were acting as if serving God in a way that was pleasing to Him was an unfathomable burden. This example isn't the only one. The pattern of questioning God continues throughout the entire book of Malachi. Malachi 3:13-15 reiterates how much of a chore God's service was to the priests:

Listen to "Connecting with Malachi—Part III" as author Jason Hayes discusses some additional implications from the Book of Malachi. Your group leader will send it to you via e-mail.

"'Your words against Me are harsh,' says the LORD. Yet you ask: 'What have we spoken against You?' You have said: 'It is useless to serve God. What have we gained by keeping His requirements and walking mournfully before the LORD of Hosts? So now we consider the arrogant to be fortunate. Not only do those who commit wickedness prosper, they even test God and escape.'"

The priests had decided that serving the Father was not only a chore, but it also was a bad decision. By their comments, they showed that they doubted the justice of God and questioned if God really knew what He was doing. Their value system had swung so low that they were jealous of "those who commit wickedness."

Have you ever felt like serving Christ was a burden? When?

What contributes to that attitude?

"What a burden." I don't think I've ever said this out loud about the things of God, but I know my mind has probably wandered there a few times. Have you ever thought similar things? It may not have been quite so clear and concise, but it certainly is easy for us to become a "victim" or even a "martyr" in our own minds, isn't it? When we think about all that we're called to do in a walk with God it can become a bit overwhelming. Our walks require time, emotion, passion, commitment, and more. Just take a minute and think of all that we're called to do as Christ followers. Here are a few to get you started:

- Treat others as you would have them treat you.
- Know the Word of God and use it each day.
- Forgive your enemies.
- Help people.
- Give thanks and be joyful.
- Don't worry.
- Pray.
- Share your faith.

The most full description of what the Christian life is supposed to be like is found in the Sermon on the Mount, recorded in Matthew 5, 6, and 7.

- Be sexually pure.
- Be good friends, spouses, and parents.
- Tithe.
- Be active in the church.
- Tame your tongue.

As you can see, we are given many commands that are quite demanding. Although we aren't saved by our actions, we are called to be faithful in them. Think about the commitment that it takes to get up 30 minutes early so you can study the Bible and pray. That's no easy task, right? Or think about the emotional energy that is consumed when you care for others or share your faith. It's draining at times, isn't it? What about how hard it is to be nice to people who are terribly rude or mean to you? This is nearly impossible at times, don't you think?

When you start thinking about all of these things, it really does seem natural to feel burdened by God and all that we are called to do. And while the idea of following God certainly isn't easy, we must be cautious or we'll find ourselves in the same mindset that plagued the priests. Faith is hard and following God is a challenge, but let me make one thing clear: God (and living for Him) should not be seen as a burden. Hard? Yes. Demanding? Absolutely. Consuming? Certainly. But burdensome? No. Not according to Scripture.

What are some ways you might be able to stop seeing serving God as burdensome?

What does that attitude communicate to others around you?

Peter posed a question to Jesus regarding the burden of following Him in Matthew 19:27-30: "Then Peter responded to Him, 'Look, we have left everything and followed You. So what will there be for us?' Jesus said to them, 'I assure you: In the Messianic Age, when the Son of Man sits on His glorious throne, you who have followed Me will also sit on 12 thrones, judging the 12 tribes of Israel. And everyone who has left houses, brothers or sisters, father or mother, children, or fields because of My name will receive 100 times more and will inherit eternal life. But many who are first will be last, and the last first.'"

Look in Malachi 2:17:

"You have wearied the LORD with your words. Yet you ask, 'How have we wearied Him?' When you say, 'Everyone who does evil is good in the LORD's sight, and He is pleased with them,' or 'Where is the God of justice?'"

Isaiah wrote during troubled times. He saw the Northern Kingdom of Israel fall and be taken captive. Judah, the Southern Kingdom, was also attacked. Yet Isaiah's message was one of hope in the future, when the Messiah would come.

As we see here, if anyone is wearied in the relationship between God and man, it is God Himself. And if there's ever been a text that should bother us, it seems that this one should. Not one of us likes to think of our lives as something that harms or hurts the Father. We must be quick to remind ourselves of God's sacrifice for us before we think of any "sacrifice" that we think we've made for Him. Isaiah 43:22-26 reminds us:

"But Jacob, you have not called on Me, because, Israel, you have become weary of Me. You have not brought Me your sheep for burnt offerings or honored Me with your sacrifices. I have not burdened you with offerings or wearied you with incense. You have not bought Me aromatic cane with silver, or satisfied Me with the fat of your sacrifices. But you have burdened Me with your sins; you have wearied Me with your iniquities. It is I who sweep away your transgressions for My own sake and remember your sins no more. Take Me to court; let us argue our case together. State your case, so that you may be vindicated."

God is saying that you and I have no reason to use our energy level or supposed "exhaustion" as an excuse for our lack of obedience to God. That makes me want to crawl under a table. How many times have we said, "I just don't have the energy for that," as an excuse for not living in obedience to Him. Now don't get me wrong, I do believe that God desires for us to be balanced in our lives and wise in agreeing to the commitments that we have. But we also need to make sure that we aren't using this "out" as a crutch for disobedience.

Not only do we use a lack of energy as an excuse out of obedience, but we are also often guilty of misdirecting the energy that we do have. In a way, the misuse of our energy is as much of a blemished offering before God as any other issue that we've discussed thus far. When it really gets down to it, it's important for us to be reminded of all that God has done for us. I believe the more we focus on the things of Him, the less we focus on ourselves. Consequently, our pity parties become fewer and farther between. Be reminded that God, in the form of Jesus, took our sins on the cross all the while remaining sinless. When you think about that, our minor inconveniences just don't seem that significant, do they? I'm really thankful for that.

How can dwelling on Christ remove the feeling of burden associated with your relationship to God?

In what other ways might your life change if you spent more time meditating on the sacrifice of Christ?

But there's something else here, too. So many times we direct our spiritual lives toward what we have left behind. We've left behind the pursuit of riches. We've left behind relationships. We've left behind our hopes and dreams, and we've done so for the sake of following Christ. If all we ever do is focus on what we've lost, then it's no wonder that living fully for Jesus feels like a burden. No wonder we get tired. After all, if you walked around looking backward all the time you can bet your neck would really start to hurt.

And it's true—a part of the Christian experience is about loss. You find it all through the Gospels—people losing their families, losing their riches, losing their prestige, and in many cases losing their lives. That seems to be what Jesus was getting at when He said:

"If anyone wants to come with Me, he must deny himself, take up his cross daily, and follow Me. For whoever wants to save his life will lose it, but whoever loses his life because of Me will save it" (Luke 9:23-24).

Following Christ involves loss. Jesus doesn't deny that fact. But this passage isn't really about loss; it's about gain. Loss is simply the means we must walk through to get to the gain. In the end, Jesus isn't saying, "Lose your life." He's saying, "Save your life! Please, save your life! Loss is only the means to gain."

There's energy and joy that comes from that fact. We can live confidently knowing that when Jesus asks for sacrifice, He replaces whatever has been sacrificed with something better. And that truth not only makes us confident in God's plan for our lives; it enables us to move forward in our walk with Him with focused intensity and renewed zeal. We can live a life filled with joy and hope for what's ahead, rather than bitterness with what's behind.

The symbol of the cross has been somewhat diminished in our day. During Jesus' time, the cross was an unmistakable symbol of public execution. The modern equivalent of Luke 9:23 might be something like, "If anyone wants to come with Me, he must deny himself, take up his electric chair, and follow Me."

REFLECTING ON MALACHI

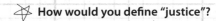

Continue reading through the Book of Malachi, focusing on Malachi 2:17–3:5. Spend some time reflecting on the following questions:

How would you define "justice"?

What did the people say about God's concern for justice in the days of Malachi?

How does the coming of the Lord relate to the administration of justice?

How does Malachi describe that day?

In conjunction with your reading in Malachi, spend some time reading Matthew 24.

What phrases stand out to you in this passage?

What similarities do you see to Malachi?

FRACTURED WORSHIP

THE BREAKDOWN OF "WHEN" AND "WHERE"

TWO GOATS WERE INVOLVED IN THE SACRIFICE ON THE DAY OF ATONEMENT. The high priest slaughtered one of the goats to sprinkle its blood on the altar. The other goat, the scapegoat, was sent into the desert to die. But before it was, the priest placed both his hands on the head of the goat and confessed all the sins of the people for the year. Then the goat was sent away to the place where sin belonged—away from the community of God.

The people were together. They were together in their sin. They were together in the anticipation of the ceremony. And they were together in the relief and celebration of God's grace and mercy for another year. After the priest completed the sacrifice they would start over, renewed and reminded that they were the people of God, the ones called out of darkness into light, ready to be His community once again.

SPRINKLERS

I'm not terribly handy around the house. It's not because I don't work hard; I do. But the projects I take on rarely come out like I intended. Just a few examples include plumbing, electrical work, carpentry, and, well, lots of other stuff. But then there's yard work. Yard work I can do.

A few years ago I decided that I was going to take on a weekend project related to the watering of my yard. I didn't have a big yard, so I thought I could take care of the problem pretty quickly. I wanted to create a sprinkler system. I know what you're thinking: *A sprinkler system? Doesn't that involve digging ditches and laying water lines?* Not for me. I had a better idea.

My simple—and yet ingenious—plan was to lay out a series of hoses and sprinklers that could water the entire lawn at the same time, thereby saving me from having to move sprinklers around every half hour. Lawn is watered; I do less work. It was a win-win.

In preparation, I bought several hoses, sprinklers, and an amazing device called a splitter. The splitter was necessary because with only one exterior faucet I had to get water into several different hoses. The splitter came out of the faucet and split the water into four parts, each going to a different hose. Each hose was attached to a different valve, so you could choose whether to water one part or all four. Then each hose led to a sprinkler which would saturate its area of the yard. Do you see the genius? I could turn on one valve (not four) and water for 15 minutes (not 60).

I meticulously laid out each hose behind the bushes or under rocks so as to ensure the yard was neat and tidy. Then it was time for a test run. I turned all the valves off except for zone one. And there it went! It was beautiful. The water came out perfectly and it watered its area just as planned. Next I closed that valve and moved to zone two. After making a couple of adjustments to the position of the sprinkler in zone two, it was set as well. The remaining two zones went off without incident, and I felt like I was on the verge of the watering promised land.

That was until I turned all the valves on. With all the calculating and planning of my super-duper watering plan, I had failed to account for one thing—pressure. Instead of the water bursting forth onto the dry and thirsty ground, I had four tiny little water fountains across my lawn. Seriously, if I had spun on my head and spit it would've dispersed more liquid. All because of the water pressure.

Most lawn experts agree that a healthy lawn needs at least one inch of water per week.

Here's the point: Often we spread ourselves so thin that we lose sight of what's really important. I added so many paths for the water to disperse that I kept any one sprinkler from doing a good job. The same thing is true in our lives. We disperse ourselves freely, sometimes to worthy causes and sometimes not, but more times than not, we leave little margin in our lives when it comes to the church. We are too tired, too emotionally spent, and too overextended to give ourselves to the body of Christ. This affects our serving, our giving, our emotional investment, our corporate worship, and more..

Do you ever feel spread too thin? Do you think God wants you to feel that way?

Do you have difficulty in saying no to things? Why?

How can saying no be a spiritual activity?

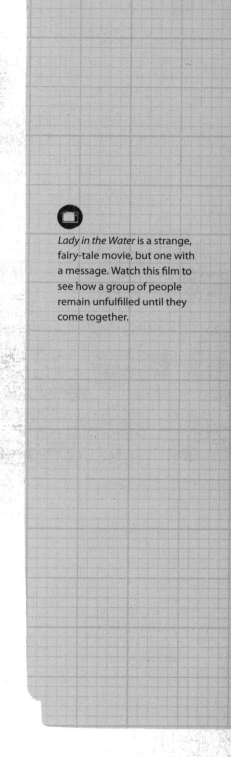

Lady in the Water is a strange, fairy-tale movie, but one with a message. Watch this film to see how a group of people remain unfulfilled until they come together.

The priests' decisions to offer blemished sacrifices in Malachi's day didn't just affect them. As the priests, they were meant to represent the people before the Lord; their actions as individuals had far-reaching corporate effects. They were called not just to be committed to the Lord, but also to be committed to their communities of faith. Our community of faith is the church. What one of us does, or does not do, doesn't just affect us; it affects the church. And the church is often the end point of our negligence, the group that deeply feels the brunt of our own blemished sacrifices.

THE IMPORTANCE OF THE LOCAL CHURCH

The church is not a building of bricks and mortar. Instead, it's the body of Christ functioning together to provide communion with one another while glorifying God by its existence. Maybe it's at this point when you start measuring that definition of the church against your past experiences. And when you compare the two you don't exactly get warm fuzzies reminiscing over the "biblical fellowship" you've

The Acts of the Apostles is the fifth book in the New Testament and chronicles what happened in the days following the resurrection of Christ. It's an amazing story, recorded by Luke, of how Christianity spread to the entire known world.

experienced. And it's even harder to think about the churches you've been a part of glorifying God with their existence. Let's be really honest—some of them don't. Heck, a lot of them don't. But hear this very clearly: We must not abandon the local church.

Do you see the local church as essential in your spiritual life? Why or why not?

How have your past church experiences influenced your level of passion for the church today?

Although our churches have flaws and errors, there is no question as to the importance that God places upon the church. Nor is there any question as to the significant role God intended the local church to play in the life of His people. I use the word "local" intentionally, because a person could make the argument that you can be a part of the church without going to a building or joining a fellowship of believers. In that understanding, all that's really meant by "church" is a belief in Jesus Christ. That's not what I'm talking about.

I'm talking about the local church, as described in Acts 2:42-47:

"They devoted themselves to the apostles' teaching, to fellowship, to the breaking of bread, and to prayers. Then fear came over everyone, and many wonders and signs were being performed through the apostles. Now all the believers were together and had everything in common. So they sold their possessions and property and distributed the proceeds to all, as anyone had a need. And every day they devoted themselves to meeting together in the temple complex, and broke bread from house to house. They ate their food with gladness and simplicity of heart, praising God and having favor with all the people. And every day the Lord added to them those who were being saved."

What do you see as the key elements of "church" expressed in this passage?

Which are the easiest for you to pursue? The most difficult? Why?

Throughout history, God has chosen to use the local church as the primary vehicle to spread His name and fame across the world. Don't get me wrong—I affirm parachurch ministries. I applaud missions sending agencies. I support conference and camp gatherings. But I don't condone replacing our commitment to the local church in favor of such things. Better yet, it appears that God doesn't either. If you look at the New Testament, it's impossible to avoid the significance of the local church.

Every letter was written either directly to or intended for local churches. Consider the ordinances of baptism and communion. They were to be performed in the context of the local church. In Christ's own words: "I will build My church, and the forces of Hades will not overpower it" (Matthew 16:18). In short, Jesus, along with all the New Testament writers, declared the absolute importance of the local church. But let's not stop there.

The local church's importance is also clearly visible in the Old Testament. All throughout the Old Testament the significance of the temple and tabernacle was revealed. Those were at least partial foreshadowings of the local church. And we obviously have seen the same thing displayed in the context of Malachi and the Levitical priests. So it's easy to recognize the prominence of the local church since its role undergirds all of Scripture.

Any negative experiences you've had with churches are not cause to abandon it. We can't throw the baby out with the bath water. We may be disgusted with what the church has become, but it's only become that way as a result of our unholy hijacking. We can't give up on it. I applaud what my friend Ed says about the church: "You can't love Jesus and hate His wife." But that's exactly what has happened, both inside and outside the faith.

If we can't give up on the church, what is the best way to deal with the trouble inside it?

When you meet with your small group this week, watch "One," a video short found on the *Blemished* leader kit. Remember that there's no insignificant member in the church of Jesus Christ.

R

Ed Stetzer is a champion for the local church and an advocate for the church embracing its missional identity. His Threads study, *Sent*, examines what it means for the church to do that, and what stands in its way. Find out more at *threadsmedia.com*.

Are you more prone to criticize the church or seek to bring about change inside it? Why?

If you haven't noticed, the world has decided that it is OK with Jesus, but not so OK with the church. Unfortunately, many Christians have decided the same. That's not acceptable. The Scripture says:

"Let us draw near with a true heart in full assurance of faith, our hearts sprinkled clean from an evil conscience and our bodies washed in pure water. Let us hold on to the confession of our hope without wavering, for He who promised is faithful. And let us be concerned about one another in order to promote love and good works, not staying away from our meetings as some habitually do, but encouraging each other, and all the more as you see the day drawing near" (Hebrews 10:22-25).

But if Scripture insists you be active in the local church and yet the local church around you isn't God honoring, what do you do? That's the million dollar question, right? Well, my suggestion is simple: Either find a new church, or better yet, take active involvement in helping it change. Either way, we as Christians must not separate ourselves from the local church simply because of the transgressions of its people. We are the people of the church. We must come to grips with the fact that we will be held just as accountable for our relationship to the local church as those who have turned many of us away from it.

CHURCH VERSUS CONSUMERISM

While we've already given much attention to the role of the church within Christianity at large, it's also important to examine what role it should play in our day-to-day living. It's important to be reminded of the impact the church can make in the lives of people. It's truly sad to see so many people affected negatively by the church, especially when God established it to be a place of encouragement, truth, rest, refuge, community, and commitment. The church was established to give glory to God, and one of the ways it does that is by impacting the everyday lives of Christ followers in a positive manner.

Part of that positive impact comes through receiving. From the church we receive spiritual encouragement and companionship. We receive the great comfort that we're not in this life alone, and we're not

We are unsure about who wrote the Book of Hebrews. Some speculate the author to be Paul; others claim Barnabas wrote it. Regardless, the audience of the letter was going through some sort of persecution and was considering giving up assembling and meeting together. It's a great message for the fracturing church of the 21st century.

supposed to be. Especially during trying and difficult circumstances, the church is meant to be a reminder of the invisible attributes of God's love, care, comfort, and wisdom. In the church, the invisible becomes visible through the lives of those around us. Christianity stops being an idea and starts being personal in the body of Christ.

> **List some of the other benefits that come along with being connected to a local church. When possible, look for Scriptures that support your ideas.**

It's a great blessing to think about all we "get" from the local church. It's so good, in fact, that it's tempting to get comfortable just being recipients. Maybe that's why so many people's affections have cooled for the church—all we ever think about is what we get from the church, either good or bad. But that narrow focus reveals that the consumerism of our culture has invaded our faith.

We treat the church like a fast food restaurant, demanding to have what we want when we want it. And if one church can't offer it, we don't come back. We either go down the street or we quit going entirely. Why? Because we're consumers—church consumers. Exclusively focusing on what we receive in a church context is really only looking at half of what God intended for our relationship with the church to be.

We need to be reminded that church is not the place where we solely come and get fed and ministered to. Instead, it is a place where we are to give—to give our time, talents, energy, and passion in order to serve and meet the needs of others. We do this for people both inside and outside the church as we utilize our gifting from God. Through giving we stop being consumers of church. We stop going to church and start being the church.

> **Read 1 Corinthians 12:12-27. What is meaningful to you about Paul's illustration there?**

In *Simple Church*, Thom Rainer and Eric Geiger argue that church has become too complicated. Simple churches thrive by taking four ideas to heart: Clarity. Movement. Alignment. Focus. *Simple Church* examines each idea, clearly showing why it is time to simplify.

What are the implications of comparing the church to a body?

The church at Corinth was a gifted, though often misguided, group of people. Paul's body metaphor served to remind them to not value one person over another and to see each Christian as essential for the church to be what it was meant to be. Paul employed a similar metaphor in Romans 12.

In Paul's use of the physical body to illustrate the various gifts within the body of Christ, one specific thing stands out to me—everyone has a role. No member in the illustration got to do nothing while the others picked up the slack. Unfortunately, too many of us are guilty of using the church to meet our needs while not participating in it in order to help meet the needs of others. We look to the church to be served, not to serve others. That's got to change.

How much do you give of yourself to the local church? What are some things that need to change in your life to free you up to give more?

CORPORATE WORSHIP
Malachi 1:10 makes a startling statement in regard to all this talk about our corporate identity as the church. God declares:

"'I wish one of you would shut the temple doors, so you would no longer kindle a useless fire on My altar! I am not pleased with you,' says the LORD of Hosts, 'and I will accept no offering from your hands.'"

That's pretty cutting. One biblical commentator puts it this way: "God, speaking in the first person, desired for someone to shut the temple doors, thereby preventing the useless, insincere presentation of sacrifices. It would be better to stop all sacrifices than to offer insincere offerings."[25] We see something similar in Isaiah 1:11-15.

The temple was meant to be the place where the people of God corporately met with Him. That's what we call a worship service today. I wonder if God, when He considers the way in which we come to worship Him, might have a similar suggestion. The Levitical priests were guilty of offenses both inside the temple (related to the sacrificial system) and outside of it (marrying foreign wives, etc).

In the same way, we also are often guilty of offenses before God both inside and outside our church buildings. Ultimately, our attitudes, motives, priorities, and inaction come together in a half-hearted, obligatory attempt at worship. What is meant to be the culminating experience of the Christian life, the moment when we get lost in our love for God, instead becomes a moment for us to check our watches and roll our eyes.

How often are we guilty of coming to our times of corporate worship with insincerity? That's the word that really stands out to me in the verse above. Oh, we show up just like the priests did. Their attendance wasn't in question; neither is ours. But *how* do we show up? I wonder if some of the ways I approach my corporate times of worship aren't just as displeasing to the Father as those of His followers centuries ago.

Have you ever considered spending significant time getting ready spiritually for corporate worship? Why or why not?

What value could there be in a time like that?

Think about the state of mind that you often bring with you to your times of worship. I struggle to believe that God is pleased when we argue with our friends or spouses on the way to church, and then immediately throw up a façade as if nothing is wrong when we pull into the parking lot. What about when we sing or read liturgy? I doubt God is pleased when we mindlessly repeat lyrics or creeds without even taking time to consider what we're saying. And then there are those times when you stayed out so late that you barely even stay awake, much less focused, in your times of corporate worship.

Our worship experience is pretty laughable when you start to think about it:

- Acting like you are reading the Scripture while secretly reading the bulletin.
- Thinking more about what's for lunch and when you'll be dismissed than what the pastor is talking about.

> "'What are all your sacrifices to Me?' asks the LORD. 'I have had enough of burnt offerings and rams and the fat of well-fed cattle; I have no desire for the blood of bulls, lambs, or male goats. When you come to appear before Me, who requires this from you—trampling of My courts? Stop bringing useless offerings. I despise [your] incense. New Moons and Sabbaths, and the calling of solemn assemblies—I cannot stand iniquity with a festival. I hate your New Moons and prescribed festivals. They have become a burden to Me; I am tired of putting up with [them]. When you lift up your hands [in prayer], I will refuse to look at you; even if you offer countless prayers, I will not listen. Your hands are covered with blood'" (Isaiah 1:11-15).

 One of the foremost experts on worship in the last century is Robert Webber. Perhaps his best known and most influential resources is *Ancient-Future Worship: Proclaiming and Enacting God's Narrative.*

- Texting with others during worship about what you're doing later that day.
- Staring at someone to whom you're attracted.

Seriously? These moments are supposed to be climactic, a foretaste of eternity, and we treat them like they're a lecture series about the tax code. We need to understand the magnitude of an encounter with God. He is, after all, the Creator and Sustainer of the world. I personally believe that some of us need to reacquaint ourselves with a reverence toward Him.

Although I affirm the ideas that God knows us personally and loves us more than anyone, Jesus is not our homeboy. And God is not our copilot. Through the redeeming blood of Jesus, we find communion with the Father. He knows us deeply and we can know Him deeply as well. However, we are not coequals with God, and our relationship with Him is different than any human relationship we may have. All too often we treat God just like He's our buddy we hang out with on Friday night. But our buddy is not omniscient, omnipresent, or omnipotent. Again, we can know Him intimately, but we need to be cautious in devaluing the greatness of God because it affects us in many ways, including our approach toward corporate worship.

Based on your approach to corporate worship, how much do you respect your relationship to God? Why do you say that?

Listen to "Breathe" by Amy Courts on the *Blemished* playlist. Your leader will send you the whole playlist via e-mail, or you can find it at *threadsmedia.com/media.* Use these songs as the background music for your study.

THE REST OF THE STORY

Malachi is a rebuke. It's a rebuke to a group of people who had fallen into routine and no longer realized the significance of their actions. It's a rebuke to those of us who equate Christianity to citizenship and move no deeper than set, habitual patterns. But Malachi is also about hope. As the book draws to a close, there is a reminder to the faithful. In Malachi 3:1–4:6 we see that God will clearly make a distinction between the wicked and godly and that His justice will prevail. We also see the continued foreshadowing of John the Baptist and then our Messiah, Christ Jesus.

But take special note of Malachi 3:8-12. It says in verse 10:

"'Bring the full 10 percent into the storehouse so that there may be food in My house. Test Me in this way,' says the LORD of Hosts. 'See if I will not open the floodgates of heaven and pour out a blessing for you without measure.'"

That's an interesting verse because at first reading it contradicts other places in Scripture that clearly tell the people of God *not* to test Him.

But here it appears that God is encouraging the people and priests of Israel to explore the fullness of His character. He's inviting them to pull a 180, to reverse their patterns of carelessness and religious complacency. In so doing, God invited them to see what life with Him is really like. It can be, says God to the people, a life of abundance, protection, and blessing. It seems like Jesus said the same thing (cf. John 10:10).[26]

And as we conclude our study of Malachi, I would encourage you to consider doing something similar—not necessarily testing God, but rather exploring the fullness of His character. The priests only knew a God who was forced to respond to their sin. God was telling them there was a better way to live in relationship with Him. He wanted to relate to people inside of their loving obedience.

Maybe, just maybe, we need to do the same. So let's take a step forward. Let's take a step toward knowing God as He responds to our obedience, not just as He forgives our shortcomings. Let me be clear and cautious—this doesn't mean He'll reward us with wealth, health, fame, or power. I have no idea how He might choose to honor your faithfulness, but it's pretty clear He will.

His plans and ways greatly exceed anything we can imagine. He is great and worthy of our praise. He is the only thing in this world that is truly awesome.

May our lives display our belief in that kind of God. May we be seen as "unblemished offerings" before God and a world that so desperately needs Him.

Amen.

Listen to "Connecting with Malachi—Part IV" as author Jason Hayes discusses some additional implications from the Book of Malachi. Your group leader will send it to you via e-mail.

REFLECTING ON MALACHI

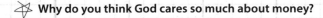

Continue reading through the Book of Malachi, focusing on Malachi 3:6–4:6. Spend some time reflecting on the following questions:

✧ **Why do you think God cares so much about money?**

✧ **What does our generosity reveal about our relationship with God?**

✧ **What feeling does the end of Malachi leave you with?**

✧ **If you had to sum up the whole idea of the message of Malachi, what would it be?**

In conjunction with your reading in Malachi, spend some time reading Revelation 22.

✧ **What phrases stand out to you in this passage?**

✧ **What similarities do you see to Malachi?**

NOTES

END NOTES

SESSION 1

1. From the title of Dan Kimball's book, *They Like Jesus but Not the Church: Insights from Emerging Generations* (Grand Rapids: Zondervan, 2007).
2. *The Zondervan Pictorial Encyclopedia of the Bible, Volume 1*, ed. Merrill C. Tenney (Grand Rapids: Zondervan, 1976), 845-846.
3. *The MacArthur Study Bible*, ed. John MacArthur (Nashville: Word Publishing, 1997), 1359.
4. William Sanford LaSor, David Allan Hubbard, and Frederic William Bush, *Old Testament Survey: The Message, Form, and Background of the Old Testament, Second Edition* (Grand Rapids: Eerdmans, William B. Publishing Company, 1996), 415.
5. Ibid., *The MacArthur Study Bible*, 1359.
6. James Montgomery Boice, *The Minor Prophets, Volume 2: Micah–Malachi* (Grand Rapids: Baker Books, 1986), 572.
7. Ibid., *The MacArthur Study Bible*, 1359.
8. Ibid., *The MacArthur Study Bible*, 1359.
9. *Evangelical Dictionary of Theology, Second Edition*, ed. Walter A. Elwell (Grand Rapids, Baker Book House Company, 2001), 954.
10. Ibid., *The MacArthur Study Bible*, 1361.
11. *The Complete Word Study: Old Testament*, ed. Warren Baker (Chattanooga: AMG Publishers, 1994), 2381.
12. Ibid., *The MacArthur Study Bible*, 1576.

SESSION 2

13. Ibid., *Evangelical Dictionary of Theology, Second Edition*, 954.
14. Ibid., *Evangelical Dictionary of Theology, Second Edition*, 954.
15. Ibid., *The MacArthur Study Bible*, 1808.

SESSION 3

16. David W. Baker, *The NIV Application Commentary: Joel, Obadiah, Malachi* (Grand Rapids: Zondervan, 2006), 229.
17. Ibid., *The MacArthur Study Bible*, 1361.
18. *http://www.msnbc.msn.com/id/27518699/*
19. Ibid., *The MacArthur Study Bible*, 1363.
20. *http://www.ctlibrary.com/le/2004/fall/18.89.html*

SESSION 4

21. Ibid., *The MacArthur Study Bible*, 1359.
22. Ibid., *The NIV Application Commentary: Joel, Obadiah, Malachi*, 242.
23. *The Zondervan Pictorial Encyclopedia of the Bible, Volume 3*, ed. Merrill C. Tenney (Grand Rapids, Zondervan, 1976), 58.
24. Ibid., *The MacArthur Study Bible*, 1363.

SESSION 5

25. Ibid., *The MacArthur Study Bible*, 1362.
26. Ibid., *The MacArthur Study Bible*, 1366.

REDISCOVERING HOPE IN REALITY

JADED

MIKE
HARDER

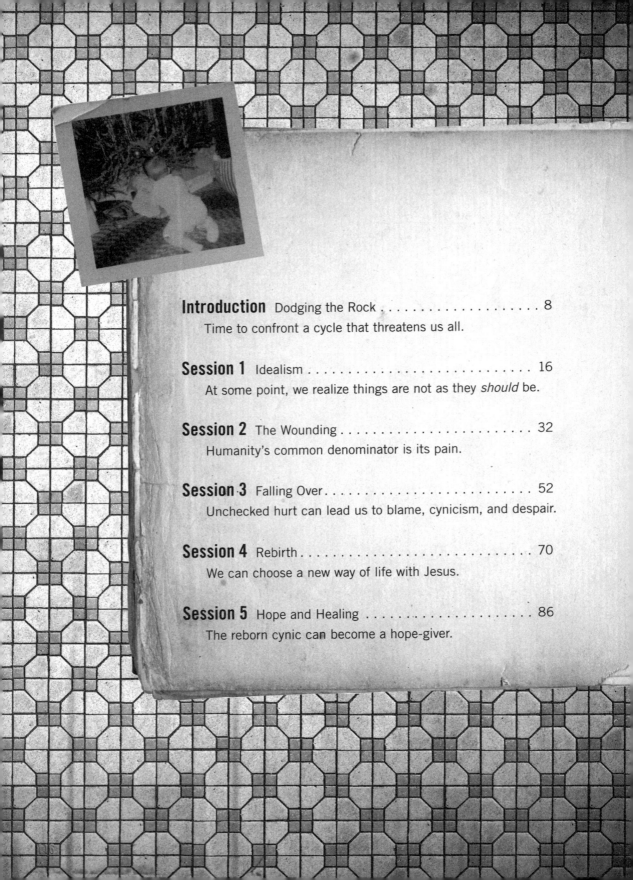

MEET THE AUTHOR

My name is Mike Harder, and I'm pretty much a normal guy who enjoys coffee (lots of coffee), wakeboarding, and several other sports. To know anything about me, you have to know the context of my life: I'm a missionary kid from Bogota, Colombia, where my parents served for twenty-eight years as church planters. I love being from Colombia, but God has called me to serve in the United States—it's my mission field. I am currently part of a new church in Nashville, Tennessee. Green Hills Church is a community that values accepting people as they are and walking with them toward maturity in Christ.

Before moving to Nashville, I earned a Master of Divinity from Mid-America Baptist Theological Seminary in Memphis, Tennessee. In addition to serving as co-pastor at Green Hills Church, I have opportunities to speak nationally through Mike Harder Ministries. In all of this, I'm motivated to make an impact on the spiritual condition and health of my generation, and I believe God can use Jaded to help make it happen. Come by and visit me at mikeharderministries.com or check out greenhillschurch.org.

JADED

Dodging the Rock

I love whitewater rafting. Last summer my dad and I went on a father-son adventure in northern Wisconsin. The first day on our week-long trip, we hit the river in a boat with two other friends looking for adventure. As we were pushing off, our river guide, Sam, told us, "Guys, you really only need to watch out for one rock."

That particular boulder—a monster the size of a small car—was appropriately named Volkswagen Rock.

We headed down river and entered the gorge, synchronizing our paddle strokes and paddling hard to the right. At first it looked like we were going to pass through easily. Then, his voice cracking with fear, Sam screamed, "Hard left! Hard left!" The current was dragging us straight toward Volkswagen Rock. Everything blurred together for a few seconds. Sam shouted. Then Sam gurgled. Water passed over us. Five grown men began screaming and our raft collided with stone. Then there was only the deafening sound of rushing water.

When I opened my eyes, I was alone in what had once been the raft. Our boat had become blue graffiti on a rock wall, the same rock wall I was pinned to by the current. I took inventory to make sure my arms and legs were still attached; then I started laughing hysterically. Other rafters were pointing at us, and my father and our friends were freaking out while being swept down river in complete defeat. I had no choice but to launch myself into the rapids and join them.

After my adrenaline normalized, a thought came to mind: As much as we try to make life work for us, eventually we get shipwrecked on the rocks. Further, those rocks that capsize our lives often come out of nowhere. Things are going along smoothly at work, in our relationships, at church, and then we suddenly find ourselves struggling to catch our breath.

The question is not *if* something like that will happen to you—it will. You will become hurt in relationships. Your job will not be perfect. Your church will let you down. The real question is, "How will you respond when you discover the huge difference between your idealistic expectations and reality?"

FEELING JADED?

Time and time again, things in life don't turn out like we planned. And when life fails to meet our expectations, we all run the risk of falling into an uncomfortable state of being we didn't plan for. We may look up one day to find that we're jaded.

Webster's defines *jaded* in two ways:
- **As an adjective,** *jaded* **means "fatigued by overwork; exhausted."**
- **As a verb, it means "to tire or dull through repetition or excess."**

Those words ring true, at least in my own life. Being jaded feels something like this: You used to be sharp—excited about life's possibilities, ready to cut a new trail in your relationships or ministry or career. But along the way, life took away that sharpness and left you dull. In terms of this study, then, I think we can define *jaded* as "having the condition of cynicism and bitterness with pain at the root."

Have you given up hope that life will get any better? If so, you might be jaded. All of us have gone through experiences that lead to becoming cynical and bitter. We haven't found the right love. We haven't landed the job. Our parents have failed us. Someone has broken our heart. Our dreams haven't come true. Add yours to the list. Many of us have been disappointed by our circumstances, but we don't have to remain there. There is life—*good* life—even after our ideals collide with reality. I think together we can find the way out of disillusionment, through reality, and back to hope.

IS GOD EVER DISAPPOINTED?

Hitting a jaded state can feel pretty lonely. There's one thing for sure, though: You are not the first to experience disappointment. The Bible deals with all kinds of people who faced disillusionment and frustration, and it offers countless stories of heartache and disaster. Surprisingly enough, the One who has encountered these things most in Scripture is God Himself. Throughout the Bible, He has dealt with failures of the people He loves. Although it is easy to think that God is untouchable, unreachable, and removed from everything here on earth, the Bible paints a very different picture.

The God we see in the Bible is an emotionally interactive being who genuinely feels emotions similar to our own. He has become injured emotionally through the actions and behavior of His children. This idea is not an example of us projecting our emotions onto God; instead, it's understanding that our emotions are a reflection of who God is. After all, we were created in His image. Even God can become discouraged. Why? It's because He has given us choices, and He has high hopes for what we will do with those choices. He wants us to achieve His blueprint for abundant life. The problem comes when we put aside His plan and pick up our own plans for what we think will make us happy.

THE PURSUIT OF HAPPINESS

Everyone wants to be happy. I know I do. In fact, most of the major life decisions I make are because I think the solution I choose will bring me greater happiness than my current situation does. I may try to get a job that pays more because I think the prestige and success and money will make me happier. I may try to date because I think having that person will make me happy. I have left a job and a city and a relationship—all because I thought it would make me happier. I have consistently found myself tying circumstances to happiness.

One time I thought that a dream car would make me happier (or at least my achievable dream car; there is no way I could afford an Aston Martin). So I went out and bought it—an Infinity G35. I talked myself into it because, after all, I was single and didn't have a family or debt. But guess what? After three months, I was disappointed to realize that my G35 was, well, just a car. Plus, every time a rock cracked my windshield, I wished I had a cheaper vehicle so I wouldn't have to pay to replace it and continue maintaining the look of my nice car. (Am I the only one who does stuff like this?)

For you, it may not be a car. It may be your relationships, your job, or some kind of addiction; but we all make choices in the hopes that they'll make us happy.

What are you counting on right now to make you happy?

What's one decision you made recently thinking it would make you happier?

Wanting to be happy in and of itself is not a problem. But what happens when a scheme to become happy fails us? What happens when we're disappointed? What happens when we're wounded by the very thing we thought would make us happy?

When our dreams don't come true, we can become disillusioned. Depending on how we deal with that disillusionment, we can become cynical. Cynicism, over time, makes us jaded. And once we've become jaded, we refuse to invest ourselves in life, and we're left with only despair. I have seen this cycle over and over again. Most of the time, we get stuck in cynicism. But there are some things we can do to move out of the cycle and into hope:

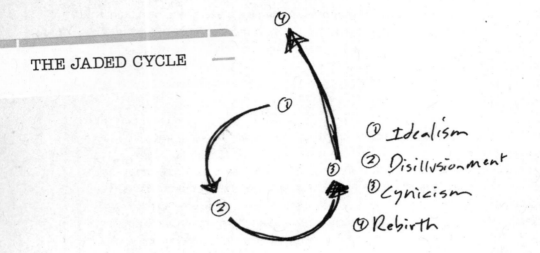

① Idealism
② Disillusionment
③ Cynicism
④ Rebirth

HURTING OURSELVES

Let's look at God's example. Through His commitment to a relationship with humanity, He has opened Himself up to every possibility of disappointment. Throughout history, God has revealed His heart as He called people to serve Him. But from the beginning they turned their backs on Him. In Genesis, we see that God created this world as a good place for people to live in relationship with Him. But humanity, starting with Adam and Eve, turned away.

When Adam and Eve chose to disobey God, they brought pain into the world. Pain is an innate consequence of sin. I used to think the consequences of sin were either given out directly by God as He zapped us when we did bad things or they were saved up until God could beat us over the head with them after we were dead. It was one of my greatest fears as a kid—that God would show all my worst stuff on an enormous TV screen in heaven. (In fact, they actually showed a video about that in my youth group. Talk about frightening!) But that version of what happens when we sin is not exactly accurate.

God is not sitting up in heaven waiting to zap us for the bad stuff we do, but the effects of our bad choices *do cause* a lot of pain. When we go against God's plan for our lives and the world, we hurt ourselves by the very choices we make. Even when people seem to "get away" with doing wrong, they aren't actually getting away with anything. Sin brings pain to us and those around us sooner or later.

Think of a time when someone let you down. What was that like?

How do you think God may have felt when Adam and Eve deliberately turned against Him in the garden of Eden?

Think about a time when you disregarded God in your own life. How did He respond to you?

What pain have you experienced because of a choice to turn away from God?

The Bible doesn't use emotional language to describe God's reaction after Adam and Eve's choice, but it does record His response to their sin. God moved His people out of the garden and into the wild to live out the effects of their choices. The consequences of Adam and Eve's decision were disastrous. The new world that God created—which was very good—was broken. Perfect order was replaced with a sort of controlled chaos as everything right down to the animals, plants, and mountains felt the effects of their sin. It was as if God's great and beautiful masterpiece was suddenly marred by a stain that ultimately infiltrated every part.

In choosing to sin, Adam and Eve gave up their claim to eternal life and unbroken fellowship with God. Their lives were flipped upside down. The blessing became the curse; the work became the toil; the fellowship became the banishment. But there is an interesting detail in Genesis 3 that gives us more insight into the complex emotions of God. Even though humanity willfully, blatantly, and consciously chose to go against God resulting in catastrophe, we find God doing something more than punishing Adam and Eve:

"The Lord God made clothing out of skins for Adam and his wife, and He clothed them" **(Genesis 3:21).**

At the same time He was handing out discipline, God took time to provide for a seemingly insignificant need for those He loved—He covered their nakedness, thereby helping them deal with their shame.

It seems as though He is always doing things like that, doesn't it? Even when God is disciplining us, He is always thinking about our future. You could even go so far as to say that God never disciplines His children without including some element of redemption. God had a choice: He could abandon the world He had created, or He could salvage it. He chose—and still chooses—to engage with people even when they hurt Him through their disobedience. He doesn't give up; He still moves forward.

WHAT ABOUT US?

It's easy to become disillusioned when we face the fact that life is far from perfect. The effects of sin ripple throughout our world and into our lives. Things won't always turn out the way we want them to. We have hopes, and we face failures. We become wounded, then cynical, then jaded. So many people I know struggle with a jaded cynicism—including me.

Yet it's incredible to know that we have a God who is working to bring healing and hope to our world, and He will not rest until He does so.

In each session in this study, we will look at one element of the cycle that can make us jaded. I hope that you will find some freshness and renewal at the end. If we are willing to choose the kind of life that Jesus wants for us, then we don't have to be dominated by disappointment. We can instead escape from the jaded cycle and start living with a sense of hope. I don't pretend to have all the answers, but I have come to a place of renewal in some areas of my life. I believe that learning how to pass from despair to hope is necessary for everyone since we all have at least a little hands-on knowledge about despair.

If you're serious about breaking the cycle in your life, you must first decide how badly you want to do so. Before we go any further, commit to be honest with yourself as you work through this study. If you don't make this decision beforehand, it will be hard to follow through. This is a choice to look at the dark, hidden places of your life. It will be difficult, but it will be worth it.

I hope today will be the beginning of healing for you. At the end of this study, you may have even more questions than you started with, but every search for truth begins with questions. And often, the willingness to ask the questions can take us deeper in our walk with Jesus. My hope is that you will find a new quest, one that leads to hope and joy in Jesus Christ. You are at the beginning of an exciting journey.

BEFORE YOU START THE STUDY, PLEASE SPEND 15 MINUTES (OR MORE) SITTING BEFORE GOD ASKING HIM TO REVEAL WHAT'S AT THE TOP OF HIS PLAN FOR YOUR LIFE. USE THIS TIME TO OPEN YOURSELF TO HEARING FROM HIM.

WHAT IS THREADS?

WE ARE A COMMUNITY OF YOUNG ADULTS—
people who are piecing the Christian life together, one
experience at a time. Threads is driven by four key markers
that are essential to young adults everywhere, and though
it's always dangerous to categorize people, we think these
are helpful in reminding us why we do what we do.

First of all, we are committed to being responsible. That is,
doing the right thing. Though we're trying to grow in our
understanding of what that is, we're glad we already know
what to do when it comes to recycling, loving our neighbor,
tithing, or giving of our time.

Community is also important to us. We believe we all need
people. People we call when the tire's flat and people we call
when we get the promotion. And it's those people—the day-
in-day-out people—that we want to walk through life with.

Then there's connection. A connection with our church, a connection with somebody
who's willing to walk along side us and give us a little advice here and there. We'd like a
connection that gives us the opportunity to pour our lives out for somebody else—and
that whole walk along side us thing, we're willing to do that for someone else, too.

And finally there's depth. Kiddie pools are for kids. We're looking to dive in, head first,
to all the hard-to-talk-about topics, the tough questions, and heavy Scriptures. We're
thinking this is a good thing, because we're in process. We're becoming. And who
we're becoming isn't shallow.

We're glad you're here. Be sure and check us out online at:

THREADSMEDIA.COM

STOP BY TO JOIN OUR ONLINE COMMUNITY
AND COME BY TO VISIT OFTEN!

GET UNCOMFORTABLE:
SERVE THE POOR. STOP INJUSTICE.
CHANGE THE WORLD ... IN JESUS' NAME.
BY TODD PHILLIPS

Phillips guides you to understand how your faith in Christ and concern for the poor go hand-in-hand. As he examines God's character and perspective regarding poverty and injustice, he offers an understanding of what God calls you to do, along with practical ways to impact culture by caring for "the least of these."

TODD PHILLIPS *is the teaching pastor of Frontline, the young adult ministry of McLean Bible Church near Washington D.C. His passions are teaching the people of God and sharing the gospel with those who aren't yet Christians. He is the author of* Spiritual CPR: Reviving a Flat-lined Generation.

JADED:
REDISCOVERING HOPE IN REALITY
BY MIKE HARDER

Harder's second study with Threads walks people through the difference between our expectations of life and reality. *Jaded* offers hope to those who have been wounded by their experiences and provides concrete ways to choose hope in Christ rather than cynicism.

MIKE HARDER *is the co-pastor of Green Hills Church in Nashville, Tennessee, as well as a speaker guy and ministry consultant. Through his speaking, writing, and teaching, Mike is motivated by the opportunity to impact the spiritual condition of the people in his generation.*

THE EXCHANGE:
TIRED OF LIVING THE CHRISTIAN LIFE ON YOUR OWN?
BY JOEL ENGLE

An exploration of Romans 6, 7, and 8, this study will help you understand that the power of the Christian life is not found in yourself or religious activity, but in "exchanging" your life for the life of Jesus Christ. You'll learn how to overcome sin and personal hang-ups through a life of dependency on Christ.

JOEL ENGLE *is a worship communicator who uses his gifts to impact lives and glorify God. In* The Exchange, *Joel shares his own story of finally understanding what the Christian life is all about and learning to depend solely on Christ.*

FOR FULL DETAILS ON ALL OF THREADS' STUDIES, VISIT *WWW.THREADSMEDIA.COM.*

GROUP CONTACT INFORMATION

Name _____ Number _____

E-mail _____

Name _____ Number _____

E-mail _____

Name _____ Number _____

E-mail _____

Name _____ Number _____

E-mail _____

Name _____ Number _____

E-mail _____

Name _____ Number _____

E-mail _____

Name _____ Number _____

E-mail _____

Name _____ Number _____

E-mail _____

Name _____ Number _____

E-mail _____

Name _____ Number _____

E-mail _____